Linlithgow 1851: A Moment in Time

Alex Adamson

Linlithgow 1851: A Moment in Time

About the author

Alex Adamson lives in Linlithgow with his wife and two children. He is the Buildings at Risk Project Manager at the Scottish Civic Trust. He is an active member of Linlithgow Civic Trust and co-author of 'Linlithgow - Architecture and History of a Scottish Royal Burgh'. He has an honours degree in history from Edinburgh University and a post graduate diploma in European Urban Conservation from Dundee University.

Alex was bridge columnist for Scotland on Sunday for five years and has had bridge articles published in a number of magazines

I would like to thank family and friends who have helped me through the process of writing this work. They have saved me from many errors and helped direct me to useful information. I would especially like to thank Abigail for the countless hours she has spent on the design and formatting, turning a manuscript into a book.

Front cover

The Dawsons, a prominant Linlithgow family stand behind their Kellie in-laws, in a photograph thought to have been taken in June 1868. The white bearded John Dawson stands beside his wife Euphemia. Beside her stand their son, Adam, and one of his sisters, either Frances or Jane. The young woman in front of Adam is his wife, Helen (nee Kellie), holding their son John Kellie Dawson. The lady in the background is unidentified but there is a suggestion that it could be a nanny or similar. Copyright Russ Sims.

Book design by Abigail Daly | abigaildaly@yahoo.co.uk

Contents

INTRODUCTION

Introduction

The main focus of this work is the parish of Linlithgow in the year 1851 through the picture of the people provided by the census of that year. More particularly, it comes from a desire to answer the questions: who lived in Linlithgow at that time, what did they do and where did they come from?

The mid nineteenth century was a time of great change; social, political, technological and economic. New industries and ways of life were superseding the old. The Linlithgow 1851 census gives us a snapshot of life in one place at one point in time. In isolation this is interesting but lacking in context. To put it another way, to understand the town in 1851 it is important to ask where had Linlithgow come from? How was it changing? And what were the outside forces that were shaping it?

There are a number of other 'snapshots' in the sixty years leading up to 1851 which help us to understand how the town and parish had been developing. The first of these is the Statistical Account of Scotland. In the 1790s, Sir John Sinclair successfully realised his undertaking to document the state of every Scottish parish. To achieve this monumental task he enlisted the services of the local ministers. At this time central and lowland Scotland was very much a Presbyterian country. Since the reformation the Scots had fought repeatedly to resist the restoration of a Catholic monarchy, or the imposition of a hierarchical, Anglican style of Protestantism. In 1793 the Jacobite '45 rebellion was still within living memory and the Irish migration of the nineteenth century lay in the future. Protestant Presbyterianism largely meant the Church of Scotland. The nineteenth century was to see many splits within the church, but, at the time of the production of the Statistical Account, the ministry of the Church of Scotland had a near monopoly position. The ministry provided a body of literate men covering every part of the country. The account for Linlithgow was written by the Rev. James Dobie in December 1793, a man who, if we use his figures for congregation sizes, counted over 85% of the populace amongst his flock.

From 1801 onwards a census was held every ten years. Over time, the data gathered became more sophisticated. The 1851 census was the first to record people's place of birth, which allows a much more detailed picture to be built up of where people had come from and what jobs were associated with which places of origin. The 1841 census has been subject to study by Andrina Baillie, providing very useful information on the town ten years before our period.

In 1843 the New Statistical Account of Scotland was published. The new series followed the model of its predecessor. This was the year of the Disruption with the splitting away of the Free Church from the Church of Scotland. The role of the church was far wider than simply religion, reaching out into the provision of education and poor relief. As such, the disruption led to the creation of parallel organisations in all these fields. Churches and schools proliferated, and before long it became clear that responsibility for providing for the poor had to be transferred to the state. The information for the New Statistical Account was gathered as these events were about to unfold, and the Church of Scotland was still the unchallenged, dominant force. On this occasion, the account for Linlithgow was written by the Rev. Andrew Bell. In 1851 this native of St Andrews was 58 years old, still living in Linlithgow and gave his occupation as Minister of Linlithgow in defiance of the other ministers in the town.

Further light can be shed on the development of the economy of the town from two trade directories. These were the 'Yellow Pages' of the time, but also provided a short description of the economy and major institutions of each town, as well as a touch of 'Who's Who'. Linlithgow was covered by Pigot's Commercial Directory of 1837 and Slater's Commercial Directory For Scotland, published in 1852.

The final written source which provides an insight into Linlithgow in 1851 comes in the form of a series of four articles, published in April and May 1901 in the Linlithgowshire Gazette under the title 'Linlithgow In 1851'. These were written at a time when the characters and events of 1851 were still remembered by the town's senior citizens. The first looked at the town council, the second at the taverns, the third and fourth at the businesses operating at the time.

As well as these written descriptions, there is useful map evidence for the development of the town. In 1820 the prolific cartographer John Wood produced a detailed map of Linlithgow, including the names of many of the house owners. 1857 saw the production of the first series of Ordnance Survey maps, giving a meticulous picture of the town shortly after 1851. Some of these snapshots, or sources of information, are focussed solely on the burgh itself. Even those, such as the Statistical Accounts, which consider the whole parish, give it the bulk of their attention.

It is worth sketching out the extent of the landward part of the parish. Starting from the northern border and moving clockwise, Linlithgow parish was, and is, bounded by Bo'ness, Abercorn, Ecclesmachan, Bathgate, Torphichen and Muiravonside. The last of these is in Stirlingshire while the rest are all in West

Lothian. The boundaries have changed over time but the following map shows where they lay in the mid nineteenth century.

The southern slopes of the hills between Linlithgow and Bo'ness fall within the parish. From there, the boundary runs along to the north-east corner of the parish at Pardovan. Turning south, it runs past Little Ochiltree to Oatridge and East Binny.[1] From here the border turns to the south-west. It switches north at Cairnpapple, which lies on the Torphichen side of the boundary, and heads up, past the western edge of Beecraigs, to Cockleroy (most of which is in Linlithgow). Next, it skirts round to the south-west, incorporating Easter Carribber and Carribber Mill, as far as the Avon. The river forms the western boundary of the parish all the way back up to the boundary with Bo'ness parish, passing Woodcockdale and Linlithgow Bridge.

The landward area is therefore quite substantial. Though it is increasingly hilly towards the south, the vast majority of the parish was suitable for agriculture in one form or another and most of it was divided into farms or estates. The more elevated areas were generally more suitable for pasture than tillage.

---

1   *The Binny area was transferred to Ecclesmachan in 1891.*

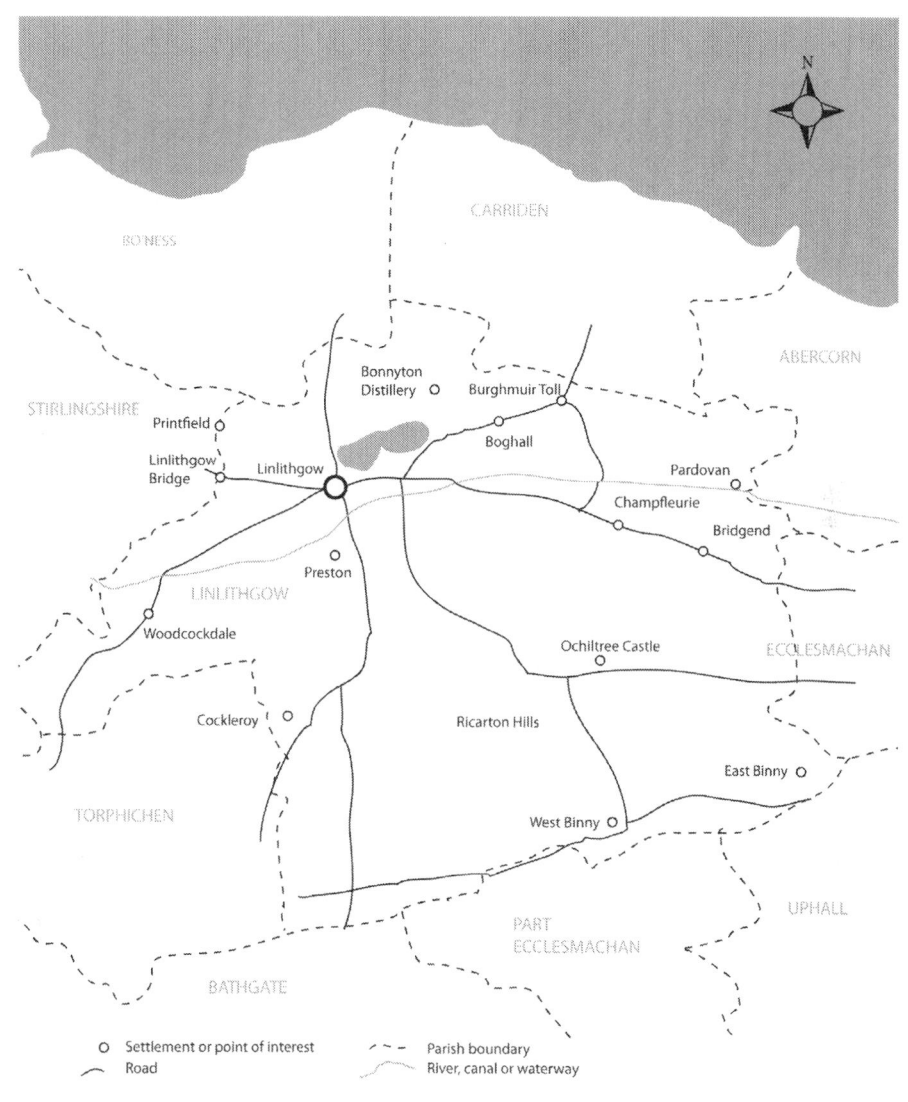

The Parish of Linlithgow in 1820 based on John Thomson's map

National Perspective

The eighteenth and nineteenth centuries saw sweeping changes to the social and economic landscapes of Britain. The major changes are often lumped together under the headings of the Agricultural Revolution and the Industrial Revolution. Though the former probably gathered pace ahead of the latter, the two fed off each other. Improved agricultural techniques and machinery increased production and reduced the need for human labour. Larger field sizes and the widespread introduction of crop rotation increased yields. Widespread drainage brought more land into productive use. Advances in chemistry led to a better appreciation of what made an effective fertiliser; in 1840 South American guano began to be imported into Britain.[2] Scotsman Andrew Meikle was the first to patent a threshing machine in 1788, while in 1826 another Scotsman, the Reverend Patrick Bell, invented a mechanical reaper. Across the Atlantic, Americans improved upon Bell's idea with Cyrus McCormick's model winning acclaim at the Great Exhibition in 1851. In 1836, Americans Moore and Hascall invented a horse-drawn combine harvester. These and other advances led to a drift from the countryside into the towns, providing the man (and woman and child) power for the new mills and factories. In some areas the process of agricultural 'improvement' was dramatic and brutal; the early nineteenth century was the period of the Highland Clearances, which saw large areas depopulated to make way for more profitable sheep farming. Many Highlanders emigrated, but larger numbers sought to build a new life in the urban areas of Scotland.

Continued industrial innovation, and the consequent reduction of the cost of production, helped drive forward agricultural improvements. Transportation in Scotland in the mid eighteenth century was slow and haphazard. A. J. Younger wrote 'In the 1760s the roads in Lanarkshire and around Glasgow were commercially unusable for the carriage of grain until they dried out in the summer time.'[3] The growing need to transport high volumes of raw materials and finished goods across greater distances led to the unmade, rutted highways of the eighteenth century being overtaken first by canals and then by the railways. Under pressure from these new modes of transport, and the increasing demands of producers and purchasers, the road network slowly improved. One key element was that many new bridges were built. Also, road provision was in part privatised through the creation of toll charging turnpike toads. Travel times and costs were slashed, which again enabled and encouraged farmers and

---

2   Brown, p212
3   Younger, p27

manufacturers to produce greater quantities more cheaply.

The need for unskilled labour to work in the new factories and to build the new infrastructure could not be met entirely by the flow of people from the countryside and highlands. The demand was in large part met by emigration from Ireland. B Collins wrote:

> 'Over eight million men women and children emigrated from Ireland between 1800 and 1921. Almost every generation of people born in the island during the nineteenth century contributed to a greater or lesser degree to this movement. Growing up in Ireland meant preparing to leave it as emigration became part of the expected cycle of nineteenth and twentieth century life.' [4]

The 1820s and 30s could be described as the wild west period of the industrial revolution. Factories were thrown up, fortunes were made and lost and the newly urbanised workforce had to endure harsh working hours and living conditions. By the 1840s the pendulum was starting to swing away from the employers and to the employees. Three Factory Acts in rapid succession improved working conditions. After Peel's Factory Act of 1844 came the Ten Hours Act of 1847, which attempted to limit daily toil. This was followed by the Sixty Hours Act of 1850, which attempted the same over the period of a week and to establish Saturday afternoon as a holiday.

In the late 1840s, the tragic famine in Ireland led to a swing away from protectionism towards free trade (in the face of bitter opposition) with the abolition of the Corn Laws in 1846. Though the main purpose was to help the starving people of Ireland, the repeal had a major impact in Britain. The cost of corn fell dramatically to the benefit of the majority of people, but to the detriment of farmers and their labourers. The cost of wheat dropped by 40% from 1841 to 1851.[5] Overall, the first half of the nineteenth century saw many key commodities fall in price. Indeed, the indexed cost of living in 1851 has been calculated to be half what it was in 1811.[6] Though this was good news for most people, there were many losers. Some groups of workers, such as handloom weavers, saw their industries almost wiped out by mechanisation. Some others, such as agricultural labourers, saw their wages remain fairly static. This was not a great period for Scotland's miners although the boom in iron working in the

---

4   Collins, p366
5   Cole, p135
6   Cole, p135. Cole gives the indexed cost of living as 174 in 1801, 164 in 1811, 115 in 1821, 111 in 1831, 116 in 1841 and 80 in 1851.

second half of the century was to drive up their wages.

During the nineteenth century Scotland moved from being a rural to an urban society. In 1801 only 21% of the Scottish population lived in settlements of 5,000 or more people. By 1851 this had risen to 35.9% as the new industrial towns and old cities swelled. By the 1891 census the majority of Scots were urban.[7] We will see later that the population of Linlithgow increased during this period, but not in the dramatic way seen in the big cities and new, or newly industrial, towns. In some ways it may seem that Linlithgow was being 'left behind'. However, there were advantages to living in a place that was developing at a gentler pace. In a study of mortality rates, Michael Flinn et al. found that: 'The period from 1832 to 1855 was to be one of the worst in modern Scottish history, with frequent, severe crises rising to a peak in 1846, and only falling away in the late 1850s.'[8] This was '...the product of the failure of municipal governments to cope with the public health problems arising from urban populations of unprecedented size and density. Urban populations grew at a pace that outran the ability of city governments to provide the essential services of housing, drainage, cleansing and water supplies.'[9] The cholera epidemic of 1832 killed approximately 10,000 people, but Linlithgow escaped unscathed.[10]

The Agricultural Revolution, the Industrial Revolution, internal migration and Irish emigration took place in incremental steps with a great deal of variation due to local conditions. The net result was to transform where people lived, the jobs that they did and the society within which they existed. Sir John Sinclair's Statistical Account was produced in the youth of Jane Austen. In 1796 she began writing Pride and Prejudice. In her world, travel, even for those able to afford a carriage, could be long and arduous. Travel over long distances was, for the majority of people, impossible. A hundred years later new cities had grown up across the country, linked by thousands of miles of railway, the Edwardian period was at hand and the birth of the modern world in the crucible of the First World War. 1851 lies at the heart of this period – mid way between the Statistical Account and E. M. Forster's 'A Room With A View'. This was the age of Dickens. In 1850 he published his eighth novel, David Copperfield, and in 1852 he began the serialisation of 'Bleak House'. Where Miss Austen paints a picture of a slow paced, rural Britain, Charles Dickens' describes a depressing, industrialised land where the ten year old David Copperfield is required to work in a factory.

---

7   Flinn, p313
8   Flinn, p371
9   Flinn, p371
10   Flinn, p371

1851 saw Britain in confident mood. The Great Exhibition, in the magnificent Crystal Palace, celebrated the progress that the nation had made, her leading place in the world and optimism for the future. The Times described the year as one of 'unexampled prosperity'.[11]

---

11   Cole p151

CHAPTER ONE
THE ROAD TO 1851

Linlithgow at the End of the Eighteenth Century

By the end of the eighteenth century Linlithgow had a long and illustrious history behind it. There is no record of when the burgh was created. However, it is clear from a charter of David I that it predates 1138, making it one of the oldest in Scotland. Edward I had seen the area to be of such significance that he built a castle there in 1300 and spent the winter there in 1301. He set his masons to extend and reconstruct much of the castle in 1302, strengthening the defences.[12] In 1424 James I set in train the construction of the palace. With further additions and reworking by most of his Stewart successors this project was to continue for another two hundred years. It was at Linlithgow Palace that James V was born in 1512 and there that his mother, Queen Margaret, waited in vain for the return of James IV after the disaster of Flodden. In 1526 Linlithgow Bridge saw a battle between the armies of the Earl of Angus and the Earl of Lennox as each sought control over the young James V. 1542 saw the death of James V and the birth, again in Linlithgow Palace, of his ill-starred daughter, Mary Queen of Scots. In 1570 Linlithgow was once more at the centre of national events with the assassination, by the rival Hamilton family, of James Stewart, Earl of Moray and Regent for another child King, James VI. With the union of the crowns in 1603 the Palace gradually fell out of use. The new north range of 1624 was built for a hoped for visit by Charles I that never came to pass. With the great and the good playing out their dramas on other stages, Linlithgow carried on quietly as a county town, a market and the centre of a local community.

In 1793 the Rev. Dr James Dobie penned his description of the parish of Linlithgow. He ranked Linlithgow as 'fifth amongst the Scottish boroughs.' At that time, the town was essentially the High Street of three quarters of a mile running past St Michael's Church and the long derelict Palace. Running back from each property in the High Street were the strips of land, or riggs, that characterise mediaeval Scottish burghs, giving it the effect often described as 'herring bone'. The Wood map shows that this pattern was still largely intact in 1820. James Dobie describes the High Street as follows:

> 'The street, towards the East, is broad and airy; about the middle, contracted and gloomy: as one goes westward, it again enlarges itself. Many of the houses have, it must be owned, a mean aspect, and exhibit striking symptoms of decay. Several, however, have lately been rebuilt, and other operations of a familiar kind are now going forward; so that, in process of time, the whole may be

---

12   *Dennison & Coleman, p17*

expected to assume a modern and more elegant appearance.'[13]

Some of the new buildings of this time still survive, such as:

52 High Street (now Bar Leo and Livingston's Restaurant)
Prior to its current incarnation this former coaching inn was the Red Lion and before that the Golden Lion. In 1851 the resident innkeeper was John Lesslie.

Annet House
In 1851 the building was split between two families. Brewer William Howison and Jean Howison had eight children. Agricultural labourer James Hill and his wife Mary lived with their grown-up daughter, Helen.

43-47 High Street (now the Alliance & Leicester and Taste)
In 1851, 43 High Street was home to coal merchant and magistrate David Henderson and his sons. Number 45 was home to corn merchant and grocer David Nicol and his wife Margaret, as well as the Aitkens: Adam (currier), Isabella and their five children. William Greenfield (saddler), Sarah Greenfield and their son John lived at 47.

52 High Street (above)

---

13   *Statistical Account, P548*

Annet House (below)

43-47 High Street (above)

The town was not the economic hub that it had been in days gone by. James Dobie says that 'Linlithgow was formerly a place of considerable trade, opulence and splendour; but from the union of the crowns, especially after the junction of the kingdoms, it declined in all these respects.'[14]

The two key aspects appear to have been the diminished significance of the town with the loss of royal usage of the Palace, and the granting of burgh status to Queensferry, the latter having been 'strenuously opposed' by the town of Linlithgow.[15] The first of these meant that less wealth was coming into the town. The second reduced the area of coastline over which the town had exclusive trading rights; formerly this had been 'from the waters of Crammond to the mouth of the Avon', i.e., the whole coastline of the county.[16] However, the picture painted by the Reverend is one of a town largely prosperous and with cause for optimism.

In 1755 Dr Webster had recorded the population of the parish as 3,296. James Dobie reported the population in 1793 as 3,221, of which 2,282 lived in the town and 939 in the country. This was a decrease of 75. James Dobie believed that over a thirty year period the population of the town had increased, though not sufficiently to compensate for the decrease in the countryside. He says that 'the parish in general is well cultivated' and that 'improvements have chiefly been made in the last 30 years'[17] and, in his closing observation, that 'agriculture is in an advanced state. From the abilities and exertion of those engaged in that line, much more may still be expected.' He was aware that the depopulation of the countryside was recognised to be a widespread phenomena across the country. Whilst specifically mentioning the impact of the amalgamation of small farms into larger units as a cause, he also notes the practice of crop rotation: a rapidly adopted strategy which brought improved yields.

The crops used depended on the soil. Two cycles are described:
- Oats, a green crop, barley, grass
- Oats, peas, barley, hay

Wheat was also mentioned as a common crop.

Agriculture was very important to the economy of the parish and forms a major

14   *Statistical Account, p557*
15   *Statistical Account, p558*
16   *Statistical Account, p558*
17   *Statistical Account, p550*

and early part of James Dobie's account. The town sat within a patchwork of farms, some of which have now been built over to produce the suburbs of the 1970s and 80s.

The separation that we expect today between rural and urban activities was much less clear in the late eighteenth century. James Dobie records that 'The inhabitants are chiefly supplied with milk and butter by people in the town, who keep from 1 to 3 cows. The number in all amounts to 108.'[18]

The town owned and ran a mill which local bakers were obliged to use. In addition, there were four other mills 'for the manufacturing of all sorts of grain' within the parish. The town's bakers not only supplied the needs of its inhabitants but also the surrounding area, with exports as far afield as South Queensferry.

Under the heading 'Trade and Manufacture' James Dobie gives precedence to the manufacture of leather and the related trade of shoemaking. He records 48 people as being involved in the curing and preparation of animal hides. These supported about 100 shoemakers producing around 24,000 pairs of shoes a year. Next listed was the wool industry. Fleeces were imported from Northumberland. Turned into thread, the wool was used as a raw material to produce stockings. There was one carpet weaver and there were 23 stocking frames in operation, of which ten were run by a Glasgow company. One stocking-weaver was reported to have 'six frames constantly at work, and produced last year 2,200 pairs.'[19]

This was the age of the enlightened factory managers; New Lanark had been founded in 1785 and would be managed by Robert Owen from 1799. James Dobie records that two tambour factories employing 36 and 50 'girls' respectively had been 'lately erected.'[20] Tambourers embroidered cloth, often muslin, by hand.

The owners of the tambour factories also took care of the morals and minds of their girls:

> 'The companies at Glasgow, for whom they are employed, allow an annual sum for instructing them in the principles of religion: with that view, attendance is given every Lord's day by two of the teachers in the town. Attention of this kind is the more laudable and requisite, as the education of the lower classes is

18   Statistical Account, p551-2
19   Statistical Account, p554
20   Statistical Account, p554

unhappily neglected.[21]

Clearly, as a minister, this was a subject close to his heart.

Further textile related employment was to be found at the Printfield and Linlithgow Bleachfield, both on the River Avon, to the north of Linlithgow Bridge. The former was founded in 1786 and had peaked at 200 staff. This was down by half at the time of the writing of the Statistical Account, but there were hopes of revival. The bleachfield was in the hands of a Mr Reed, who seems to have been something of an inventor. He had high hopes for improved efficiency as a result of a new watering machine and 'a new species of pump', both of his own devising. Mr Reed also owned a nearby flint mill supplied with raw materials from Gravesend and exporting the ground flints as far as East Lothian and Ireland.

James Dobie records three breweries and four distilleries in the parish. He comments that 'The quantity distilled here is very great.' The distillery at Bonnytoun employed 24 men.

The trades were represented on the 27 member town council, known as the 'Twenty-Seven Gods'. This name was given to them, mockingly, in 1711 by the then master of the grammar school, a Mr Kirkland, when he used it in the title of a satire describing their high-handed (in his opinion) efforts to remove him from his post. The appellation seems to have stuck, being used in the 1901 series of articles in the Linlithgowshire Gazette which ran under the title 'Linlithgow In 1851'.[22]

The trades were split into two groups; the eight which were incorporated and the seven which were fraternities. Each sought to represents their members' interests, and provide benefits, particularly for those experiencing difficulties. The difference between the two was that the incorporations were granted a trade monopoly within the burgh. The fraternities were either newer trades or ones that had been less significant in previous centuries.

They are listed by James Dobie as:

Corporations
- The smiths (metal workers)
- The tailors

---

21   *Statistical Account, p544-5*
22   *Linlithgowshire Gazette, 12th April 1901, p6*

- The baxters (bakers)
- The cordiners[23] (shoemakers)
- The weavers (on handlooms)
- The wrights (wood workers: joiners or carpenters)
- The coopers (barrel makers)
- The fleshers (butchers)

Fraternities
- The dyers
- The gardeners
- The hecklers (preparers of flax for spinning)
- The skinners
- The whipmen (carters and carriers)
- The woolcarders
- The tanners

This right of representation was to come to an end in November 1852 when the old arrangements were replaced by a council consisting of a provost, three bailies, a dean of guild, a treasurer and nine councillors.[24]

Linlithgow had a long tradition as a market town. The weekly flesh market 'anciently held on Saturdays' had been transferred to Fridays. In addition there were six annual fairs, though these were not as well attended as in days gone by.[25]

At this time, the loch was able to contribute eels, pike and perch, though in decreasing amounts, and the river supplied trout. It was noted that eels were sent as far as London.[26]

The transportation of coal from Bo'ness and the Stirlingshire coalfield kept a small number of people in employment. James Dobie's figures show that 1793 was a time of fuel price inflation, with the cost of a cart load going up from 2s 8d to 3s 5d, an increase of nearly 30%![27] This was explained as largely being due to the increase in demand; an indication, perhaps, that the industrial revolution was

---

23   The word 'cordiner' derives from Cordova in Spain, a source of fine shoe leather.
24   Linlithgow Gazette, 12th April 1901, p6
25   Statistical Account, p560
26   Statistical Account, p560
27   Statistical Account, p561 Statistical Account, p561

starting to influence daily life in Linlithgow.

James Dobie considered the number of people supported by poor relief to be 'very great' at between 80 and 90.[28] He observed that no more than a third were of local origin 'or even long resident'. The 'pretty considerable' charity funds attracted incomers from as far away as the Highlands seeking to take a share in money that he felt should more properly be distributed to those 'who have a natural interest in the parish'. It is interesting to note that he makes no mention of people of Irish origin.

For entertainment, there were two inns in the town and a number of other houses 'where persons, to whom post horses are not an object, may find good entertainment.'

The Church of Scotland dominated the religious scene. However, James Dobie reported about 430 dissenters, split between two churches: one on the edge of the town and one three miles away at Craigmailen.

The Early Nineteenth Century

The world became a smaller place for Linlithgow on the 22nd May 1822 with the opening of the Union Canal, linking Edinburgh and Glasgow by water, via the Forth and Clyde Canal (which it joined at lock sixteen in Falkirk). The Forth and Clyde was completed in 1790 and had proved to be very successful. It was thought that a linking canal would assist Edinburgh through 'the conveyance of coals (from Lanarkshire), of manure, of goods and passengers'.[29] Canals don't mix well with hills and valleys, so it was a matter of good fortune that Linlithgow lay at an appropriate elevation to make it a suitable point for a contour canal with no locks to pass on the way from Edinburgh to Falkirk.

The required Act of Parliament had been passed in 1817 and construction took place between 1818 and 1822. John Wood's map of 1820 shows that the construction of the canal was well advanced in this area at that date. Two bridges, and one proposed bridge, are marked. It is notable that at that point there were few buildings along the banks of the canal.

---

28   *Statistical Account*, p564
29   *New Statistical Account (NSA)*, p755

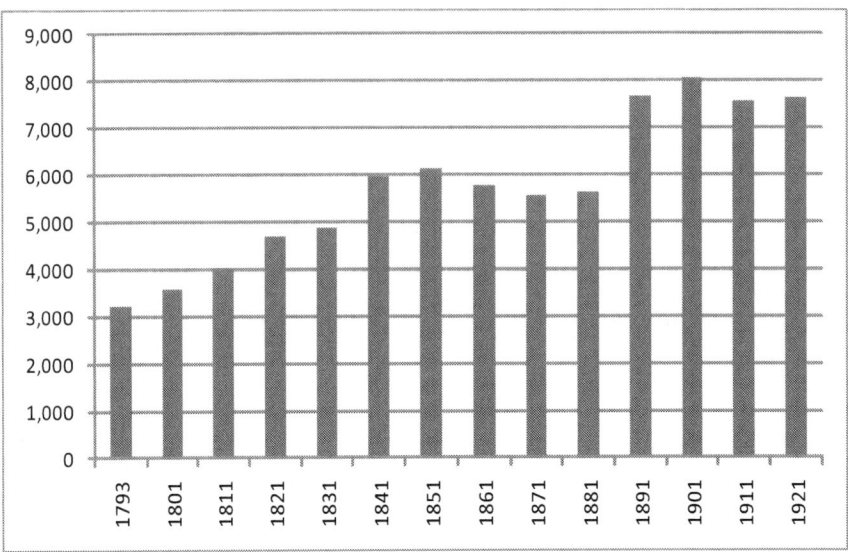

Figure 1 shows that the population of Linlithgow grew steadily until 1831, jumped in 1841, increased slightly to 1851 before declining over the following thirty years. It jumped again in the decade to 1891 and see-sawed over the next thirty years. One of the factors that brought more people to the parish in the early nineteenth century was a freak of altitude.

In medieval times Linlithgow had been a convenient overnight stop on the two day journey from Edinburgh to Stirling. By 1799 it was possible for a person to travel between Edinburgh and Glasgow by stagecoach in six very uncomfortable hours.[30] However the transport of goods continued to take days. Later in life, Provost Adam Dawson was to recall the early stagecoaches and the conditions at the time. The Edinburgh to Stirling stagecoach was:

> '...an omnibus carrying ten or twelve inside, and as many outside, and drawn by four horse...'[31]

As to the route:

> 'The roads in these days were arched to such a degree as to throw the whole traffic on to their centres, by which a couple of deep ruts, generally full of water, were formed in that quarter. Carriage horses travelled with their feet in these ruts, and few of them escaped broken legs or being lamed sooner or later.'[32]

---

30   *Younger, p29*
31   *Dawson, p25*
32   *Dawson, p25*

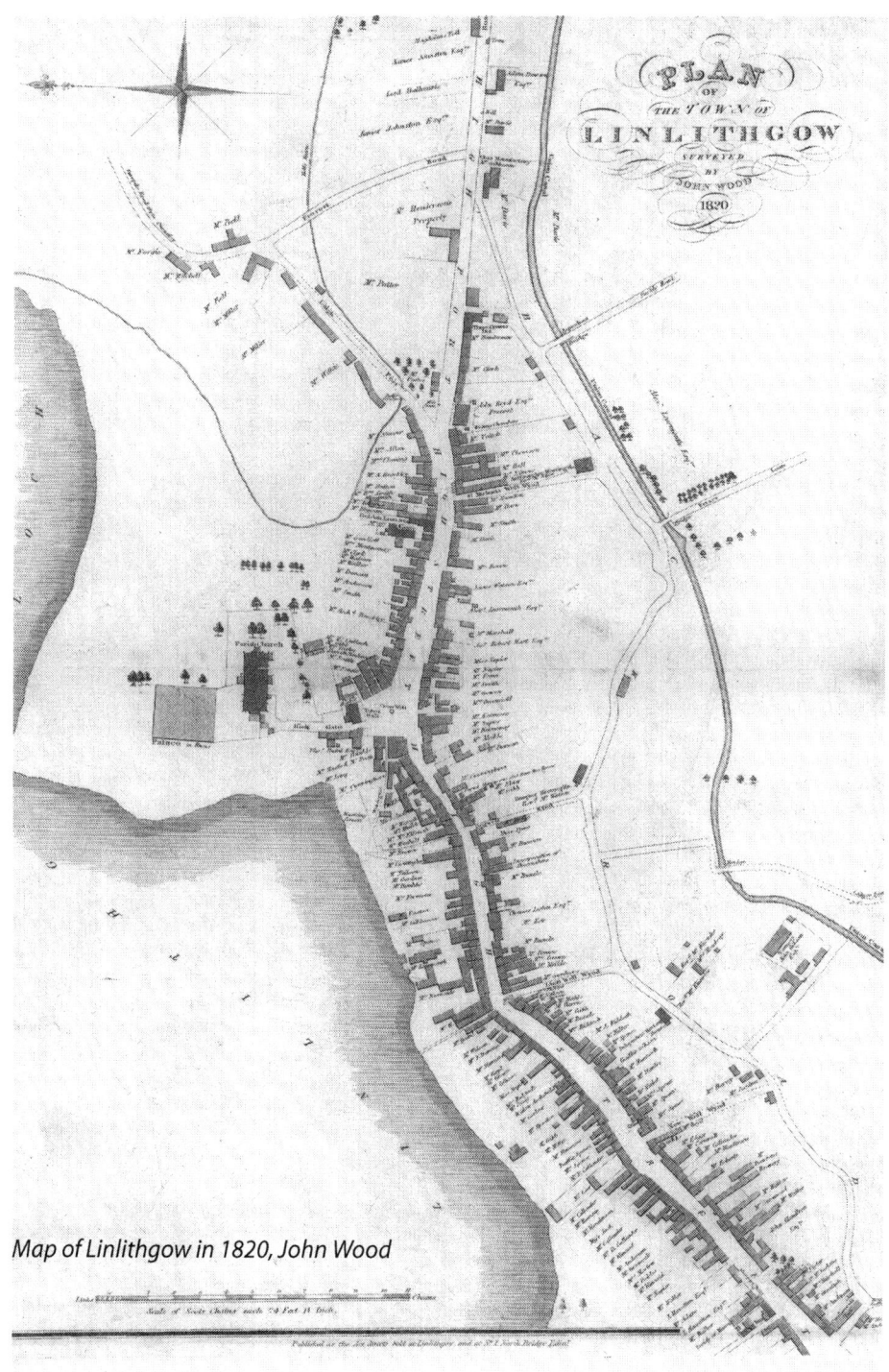

Map of Linlithgow in 1820, John Wood

The opening of the canal allowed people to travel in relative comfort. Express barges called several times a day in Linlithgow, making the journey between the cities in eight hours. Perhaps more important than the passenger journey time was the vastly increased capability to transport heavy loads easily. The canal conveniently passed a number of sites in the Linlithgow area with the potential to be quarried. This led to new quarries being opened that all required a workforce. At Kettlestoun, a whinstone quarry was opened up. At the other end of the town, the St Magdalene's whisky distillery, of which Provost Adam Dawson, father of the stagecoach reminiscer above, was a proprietor, was relocated in 1834 from its former site at Bonnytoun Farm to be near supplies of coal and coke transported along the canal.[33]

The canal brought people into the parish, firstly for its construction, and then as a labour force for the often manual jobs it created. James Handley[34] wrote that, in the early decades of the nineteenth century, Irish people were finding jobs in West Lothian as agricultural labourers and mine workers. Much of the workforce that carried out the construction came from Ireland. Probably the two most famous, or infamous, navvies who worked on the construction of the canal were Ulstermen Burke and Hare.[35]

The canal also brought money into the town coffers through the extraction of customs duties. These were payable by each barge with the amount depending on the distance it had travelled. The collection point was the canal basin at the foot of Manse Road.

A number of surviving buildings date from the first three decades of the nineteenth century.

---

33 *Historic Scotland List Description 37370 for St. Magdalene's Distillery East Barns*
34 *Handley, p30*
35 *Collins Encyclopaedia of Scotland*

129 High Street, built 1829 (above)
Home to four families in 1851 totalling 21 people: the McMurrays (shoemaker) and lodger, the Aitkenheads (shoemaker), the Hardies (shoemaker) and Janet Liddle (boot binder) and family.

The Black Bitch, 12-14 West Port (below)
In 1851 a staggering 45 people lived at 12 West Port and a further 20 lived at number 14.

78-80 High Street (above)
In 1851 this was the home of the Maxwell Muller family and their three servants. They are discussed further in Chapter 3.

159-163 High Street (below)
In 1851 159 High Street was home to Thomas and Janet Kincaid and their four children. Thomas was an ironstone miner. Margaret Christie was head of the household at 161, where she lived with her extended family of nine relations. Two families of shoemakers, the Rules and the Vines, lived at 163.

1837-41 – Dawn of the Victorian Era

1837 was a significant year across the British Empire in that it saw the passing away of the 'sailor king', William IV, at the age of 72. A father of many children, he left no legitimate heir so the crown passed to his eighteen-year-old niece, Victoria. She was to reign for the next 64 years.

For the historian of Linlithgow, it is a significant year because it saw the publication of 'Pigot & Co.'s Directory'. This book gave a brief description of each town and then listed important information in a standard format. Notable people or businesses were listed under the headings shown in Table 1. 1841 is significant because it was another census year, and because a study of the returns for the town (but not the rest of the parish) has been made by Andrina Baillie.[36] Table 1 also gives a comparison between the number of businesses in a trade recorded by Pigot and the number of people Baillie found working in the trade.

Image above: Burgh Halls, Cross Well and Cross House from an engraving possibly made in the 1830s. Copyright: B Jamieson

36   *Baillie, 'Linlithgow in Early Victorian Times', West Lothian Council Local History Library, 2006*

Even at this date, the description of the town is that 'it is chiefly formed of a single street'.[37] Pigot, or his agent, was not impressed with its condition: 'The houses have, in general, an old and decayed, but yet substantial look which indicates that the place has at a former time enjoyed greater prosperity'.[38] This suggests that if the coming of the canal had been beneficial to the town the effect had been to arrest decline rather than to advance the wealth of the town relative to its peers. It was seen as an asset to the town: 'an extensive basin of excellent masonry offers commodious accommodation to vessels trading on this canal'.[39]

Transportation was clearly much improved from the days of the Statistical Account, and there was a healthy level of competition. Pigot lists three passage boats a day to Edinburgh (leaving at 8 a.m., 2 p.m. and 5 p.m.) and two to Glasgow (at 11:40 a.m. and 2:40 p.m.). There were coaches to Edinburgh at 9 a.m. (from Falkirk), 10 a.m. (from Stirling), 5:30 p.m. (from Glasgow) and 6:30 p.m. (from Stirling). Additionally, there was one a day to Glasgow (via Falkirk) and one to Stirling. Aside from the functionally named Royal Mail, they had colourful names such as the Royal Carron, the Defence and the Soho.

As in 1793, the manufacture of leather and the related trade of shoemaking were seen to hold primacy in 1837. Pigot wrote: 'Tanning, currying, and shoemaking, may to this day be deemed to be the staple of the place. In the tannery branch there is one establishment, among several others, extensive and ingenious; it belongs to Messers Spence and Sons, who have erected a steam-engine, which is employed in the several purposes of grinding bark, heating the lakes and pumping water; the contrivance is considered worthy of the consummate in mechanical operations'.[40]

It is interesting to note that the Industrial Revolution was making its mark on this key industry and that Linlithgow was again home to at least one technological innovator. The full entry for the Spences gives the name of the company as 'Spence, Robert and Sons, High St.' In the 1851 census we find Robert (45) and his brother Alexander Spence (43), living together in the High Street, both employed as curriers and leather merchants. These seem very likely to be the 'and Sons' of 1837. Additionally, in 1851 we find another Alexander Spence (55), a shoemaker 'employing 20 men and 7 apprentices'. Like the 'brother', this Alexander was a native of the town. He lived in New Well Wynd with his wife, four sons, a daughter

---

37   *Pigot*, p641
38   *Pigot*. p641
39   *Pigot*. p642
40   *Pigot*. p641-2

and a servant girl. His oldest son was called Robert. While Robert and Alexander were common names it is tempting to suggest that the families were related. Alexander Spence the shoemaker is listed in Pigot's but the Directory gives no indication as to how many people he employed at that time. This is one of the limitations of the trade directories, but it is still illuminating to see the range of types of business and the numbers in each category.

Table 1. Entries for Linlithgow in Pigot's Trade Directory and equivalent employment numbers in 1841 reported by Baillie.

Categories in Pigot's Trade Directory	Number of Individuals / Businesses Listed in Pigot per Category	People Recorded by Baillie in 1841 Census
Gentry and Clergy	20	-
Academies and Schools	4	-
Bakers	10	17
Bank	1	-
Bookseller and Stationer	1	2
Boot and Shoemakers	16	287
Builders	3	-
Coopers	3	7
Curriers	5	43
Distillers	1	-
Dress and Straw Hat Makers	3	21
Earthenware Dealers	5	-
Fire and Office Agents	2	-
Fleshers	6	12
Glue Makers	2	3
Grocers and Spirit Dealers*	19	-
Inn	1	-
Iron Monger	3	-
Linen and Woollen Drapers and Haberdashers	6	-
Nail Makers	2	9
Painters	2	7
Saddlers	2	-
Skinners	2	6

Slaters	2	9
Stone Masons	2	90
Surgeons	2	3
Tailors	10	28
Tanners	6	24
Vintners and Spirit Dealers*	29	-
Watch and Clock Makers	2	4
Wrights	4	22
Writers (i.e. solicitors)	5	-
Miscellaneous	13	-

* The overlap between these two groups will be further discussed in Chapter 3 under Commerce and Manufacture.

The twenty 'Gentry and Clergy' included five men of the cloth, three army men, one doctor and three women. There were four churches in the town by this time: the Established Church (or Church of Scotland) at St Michael's, an Independent Church in Rose Lane, a United Secession Church in East Wynd (now Station Road), and one simply called United in Dogwell Wynd.

The Inn was the Red Lion, now Livingston's Restaurant and Bar Leo. It may seem surprising that the Star and Garter was not listed. It was in fact a private residence until 1847 when it was transformed into a hotel, taking advantage of its proximity to the railway station. Pubs are included within Vintners and Spirit Dealers.

One of the two surgeons was the famous David Waldie (1813-89), promoter of the use of chloroform, and currently celebrated in plaque form above the Four Marys.

The only blacksmith deemed worthy of a mention, Alexander Meikle, was placed in the miscellaneous group, which also included Malcolm Adam, the candle maker, Robert McCall, the rope maker, David McNeil, rag dealer, Alexander Nimmo, the vet, Peter Roberts, tobacconist, and Robert Shields, the town's one and only hairdresser.

Baillie's analysis of the 1841 census informs us about the numbers of people involved in many of Pigot's categories. Of course, four years had elapsed since the publication of Pigot's. These were not just any four years as it was during this period that the bulk of the construction work for the railway took place, bringing a massive influx of labourers. It is, however, reasonable to assume that this did not have a significant impact on the number of people practising the principal trades.

It is possible that some of the differences are due to the interpretation, or definition, of job titles. The figures seem to show that boot and shoemakers, curriers and stone masons were most likely to be employed in numbers by proprietors. Of these, the one most likely to have been inflated by the construction of the railways was stone masonry. The 1851 census would see a considerable reduction in the number of masons.

1843 – The New Statistical Account

The year 1843 permits us the first detailed look at Linlithgow Parish since 1793. The author of the New Statistical Account was the Rev. Andrew Bell, minister of St Michael's and native of St. Andrews.

Figure 1 shows that the population of Linlithgow had jumped considerably between 1831 and 1841. Andrew Bell saw this as being largely down to the influx of labour for the construction of the railway, which had opened on the 21st February 1842. In the intervening year, since the opening of the railway, he notes that 'many workmen have removed to other districts.'[41]

He seems to have considered the population that remained to be almost extraordinarily ordinary: 'There are no nobility, and but few individuals of independent fortune, residing in the parish. The people are in no respect remarkable for personal qualities.'[42]

Since 1793 the population had almost doubled. The size of the town had also increased. Where James Dobie had recorded the High Street as being three quarters of a mile it is now estimated at a mile. We may recall James Dobie's description of the High Street (see page 16). Fifty years later Andrew Bell displays remarkably similar sentiments:

'The place has an antique air, many of the houses having aspects of decayed grandeur, which testify to the power and opulence of their ancient owners. It is,

41   NSA, p178
42   NSA, p178

however, gradually changing in its look of "venerable old", as modern buildings are usurping the place of these worn-out edifices.[43]

Perhaps there is a suggestion that while the town had not fully realised James Dobie's aspirations it had, at least, kept pace.

Andrew Bell began by outlining the key features of the rural economy. Apart from 'a few acres upon hill tops inaccessible to the plough',[44] the available land was cultivated with farms ranging in size from 100 to 400 Scots acres, averaging out at 180 acres. Lime was being excavated at Silvermine, Hillhouse and Carrubbers. Two stone quarries were in operation at Kingscavil and East Binny. The latter supplied stone for Edinburgh's expansion. Compared to James Dobie's account fifty years earlier, Andrew Bell devotes remarkably little space to agriculture. Perhaps this is partly because the proportion of the population living and working on the land had decreased. What he does say is positive. In his final remarks, he observes that since the previous Statistical Account 'in agriculture, the change has been great', and that agriculture is 'as far advanced as in any district'.[45]

Turning to the town, his description shows that the picture painted by Pigot and the 1841 census still held true. He says: 'this is not a manufacturing district: but there are several species of manufacture in the town and neighbourhood. The leather trade, in its various branches, may be called the staple of the town.' Indeed, his account suggests that shoemaking was on the up. As against the 287 shoe and boot makers found in the 1841 census he says there are 343 of which 24 are masters, an increase from the sixteen master shoemakers that can be inferred from Pigot. He reports five master tanners employing 28 men (an increase of four from 1841) and nine master curriers employing 50 men (an increase of seven from 1841). All in all, he concludes, 'The tanning and currying departments are in a prosperous condition, and the shoemakers are well employed.'[46] Rates of pay varied across the professions and according to the level of experience gained. The following quote is revealing: 'A tanner, bred to the employment, receives 13s. per week, while average wages of what are called labouring tanners, that is men not brought up to the work, are only 9s.'[47] Does this show the complexity of the work, the desire for the established families to retain their primacy or something

---

43   NSA, p181
44   NSA, p178
45   NSA, p188
46   NSA, p180
47   NSA, p180

of both? Remember, the shoemakers and tanners were both represented on the town council.

In between Pigot's account of 1837 and Andrew Bell's in 1843, the shoemaking business of Alexander Morrison and Son had been established in 1839. By 1850 they employed over 50 people.

Next to be mentioned, after the leather trades, were the 'very extensive distillery... which gives employment to a number of men'[48] and the brewery. In the vicinity of the River Avon he reports a paper-mill and a large calico-printing establishment, both reported to be in full employment. The print field is recorded as being the principal employer for the people of Linlithgow Bridge. Pigot had recorded two glue-works and the same number were in operation in 1843.

Though the picture of industry and employment may appear similar to that of James Dobie's of 1793, Andrew Bell believed that: 'Since the last Statistical Account was written, considerable changes have taken place in the parish.'[49] James Dobie had listed the wool industry and two tambour factories second behind the related leather industries in his summary of 'Trade and Manufacture'. By 1843 these industries had been all but wiped out. The wool industry was gone and the factories shut down. Some tambourers clung on, working on piece rates from home: 'a number of women, principally unmarried, are engaged in sewing for Glasgow manufacturing houses. This employment can scarcely be termed remunerative, for the utmost that a female can earn, working with the most, untiring diligence from morning to night, is about 6d per day – a most miserable pittance, when we consider the toil of the over-tasked female, who, but for this, scanty as it is, would be often entirely destitute.'[50] Unlike other trades, where increased mechanisation was putting pressure on handcrafted goods, the problem for the tambourers was cheaper overseas competition. In 1869, David Bremner recorded in his book 'The Industries of Scotland' that: 'When flax-spinning ceased to be a domestic occupation female labour became very cheap in Ireland, and some of the Glasgow sewed muslin manufacturers took advantage of that circumstance, and sent agents into the north of Ireland in order to test the possibility of having work done as well and at a cheaper rate than was being paid to the Scotch sewers. The experiment proved successful, and about the year 1830

48   NSA, p180
49   NSA, p188
50   NSA, p180-181

the Irish work began to compete successfully with the Scotch.'[51]

In the 1851 census a number still survived but it is clear that their condition was becoming even more precarious.

Another lost industry from the 1793 Statistical Account is fishing. James Dobie's eels, pike, perch and trout are not mentioned in 1843. They may have been the victims of increasing industrial pollution in the loch, over-fishing or both. Alternatively, they may simply not have been deemed worth mentioning! Fishing in the loch does not seem to have been significant enough to come to the attention of the powers that be until 1879. That year, the crown objected to the catching of eels. Over the next few years the question of fishing rights was disputed with the crown stating that, as the owner of the palace and the loch, it controlled them, while the burgh claimed that its populace had enjoyed these rights 'from time immemorial.'[52]

The weekly market and six annual fairs had long been an important part of the commercial and social life of Linlithgow. In 1793 James Dobie had commented that the latter were not so well attended as in days gone by. Andrew Bell mentions them without any comment, and they are also listed in the two trade directories of 1837 and 1852, again without any further information on their success or popularity. All this allows us to conclude is that the market and fairs continued until at least this time.

The revenue of the town council was estimated at about £700 per annum. This was generated principally by property owned by the burgh, the Burgh Mills, which as we saw in the Statistical Account local bakers and farmers were compelled to use, and customs duties. Since Mediaeval times, if not earlier, Linlithgow's location close to the only crossing point of the River Avon for many miles had been used to its advantage to levy customs on passing trade. These rights were enshrined in charters, allowing it to exercise this power 'from Avon Bridge to the sea.'[53] As has already been noted, the town continued to charge customs on barges on the canal. However, the arrival of the railway was to create a new challenge to this regime. On the 4th February 1842, with the opening of the railway just seventeen days away, 'the provost, bailies and council of Linlithgow intimated to the Edinburgh & Glasgow Railway Company that they intended to levy duty on carriages and wagons crossing the railway bridge

---

51   Bremner, p353
52   Glasgow Herald, 26th March 1879, 14th April 1879 & 13th July 1881
53   NSA, p182

and passing through the station. The Edinburgh & Glasgow refused to pay and Linlithgow took the railway company to court. The case began in January 1843 and progressed through various courts with the town winning all the way until in 1853, the House of Lords found in favour of the railway.[54]

In July 1843, when Andrew Bell was writing his account, the case seemed to be going the council's way. He wrote hopefully that: 'Should it be successful, it will add immensely to the revenue, placing very ample funds at the disposal of the council for burgh purposes.'[55]

The coming of the railway, the first in Scotland, again shrank distances across central Scotland. Originally it went as far east as Haymarket Station. North Bridge (later renamed Waverley) Station was opened on the 18th June 1846, with the line being extended to it on 1st August that year. Initially there were four trains a day in each direction, though this rapidly increased. Journey times from Edinburgh to Glasgow came down to two and a half hours. During 1842 the line carried 205,268 passengers but by 1848 this had increased more than fivefold to 1,051,872.[56] With frequent services, high speeds and high freight carrying capabilities, the railway service spelt the end for the short-lived dominance of the canal. The improving road system, recorded by Andrew Bell as being in excellent condition, also contributed to the demise of the canal. As well as 30 miles of parish roads in a good state of repair, there were seven miles of turnpike roads. Turnpikes were toll levying with the proceeds used to maintain them. Like the canals, turnpikes were eventually to fall victim to the railways, with responsibility for road construction and maintenance passing to the local authorities. Horse-drawn 'omnibuses' ran from Linlithgow railway station to Bo'ness and Bathgate. As well as being beneficial to people wishing to travel between these towns and Linlithgow, they would have represented the fastest way to travel from Bo'ness and Bathgate to and from Edinburgh and other points along the railway line. The latter omnibus may not have survived the opening of the Edinburgh-Bathgate railway line on 12th November 1849. Overall, Andrew Bell concludes that 'little remains to be desired in the matter of improved communication.'[57]

Andrew Bell records a fracturing of the religious control of the Church of Scotland. Where James Dobie noted 430 dissenters in 1793, Andrew Bell notes a figure of 1,300 being given by the Church of Scotland, and a claim by one of

---

54   Thomas, p68
55   NSA, p183
56   Thomas, p63
57   NSA, p188

the secessionist ministers of a higher figure of 1,526. He acknowledges that
these figures were calculated prior to 'the recent secession', and that as such the
true figures 'cannot be distinctly stated.'[58]   Here he alludes to the events now
known as the Disruption of the Church of Scotland, which led to about 40% of
the membership and clergy leaving to form the Free Church of Scotland. This
earthquake had taken place on 18th May 1843, just weeks before Andrew Bell
completed his account.

Pigot recorded four academies and schools in the burgh of Linlithgow in 1837.
Andrew Bell records nine in the parish but since he does not list them all, it is
not clear whether this represents an increase or a decrease in the provision of
education within Linlithgow itself. In a nice link with the 1793 Statistical Account
we find that Mrs Douglas, sister of James Dobie, had founded a charity school for
girls in the town.

The number of paupers recorded in the New Statistical Account shows an
increase from 1793 from 80 or 90 to about 140.[59] While this was roughly in line
with the increase in population over the same period, Andrew Bell states that
the number had 'increased considerably within the last two years.'[60] When we
consider that Andrew Bell viewed the 6d per day paid to the tambourers to be
'scanty', we can see how desperate the lot of the poor was: average monthly
payouts were 3s 5d. At the time Andrew Bell was writing the responsibility for
poor relief still lay with the Church of Scotland through its local 'branch', the
parish church. However, the schism within the church made this unsustainable.
The government were quick to act: the Poor Law Commission reported the
following year and in 1845 the Poor Law (Scotland) Act established parochial
boards in each parish under a central Board of Supervision based in Edinburgh.
The local boards were funded through local taxation.

As in all ages, no doubt there was an overlap between the lower ranks of society
and those who were incarcerated. Linlithgow housed the County Prison and the
1841 census records twelve inmates (nine men and three women).[61] Andrew Bell
records 125 prisoners in the preceding year, which suggests that confinements
were relatively short. The enlightened regime in place attempted to reform
prisoners as well as punish them: 'in addition to the services of a chaplain, each
cell is provided with a Testament. Mr Alison the governor instructs the male

58   NSA, p184
59   NSA, p186
60   NSA, p186
61   Baillie, p27

prisoners, who cannot read or write; and his wife, the female prisoners. Many of them appear to value the instruction they receive, and some of them make considerable progress.'[62]

In his summary, Andrew Bell painted a picture of a community that had experienced change but, overall, was embracing that change to make progress: 'though various branches of trade have become extinct, there is no reason to imagine that any great decline has taken place in the prosperity of the town; population has increased, and the general comforts of the inhabitants augmented.'[63] After commenting on the improvements in agriculture and transport he finished off by observing 'much may yet be done to promote the happiness and comforts of the people.'[64]

View of Linlithgow from the canal by Hill and Adamson. Courtesy of Glasgow University Library, Department of Special Collections

---

62   NSA, p187
63   NSA, p188
64   NSA, p188

THE ROAD TO 1851

The Late 1840s

The second half of the 1840s was a period of great unrest across Britain and Europe, particularly amongst the working classes who felt short-changed by the ruling classes. They sought the vote, greater social justice and, in many European countries, the end of monarchy. The French Revolution was still, just, within living memory and elites across the continent feared a repeat on their doorstep. In Britain many of the disaffected rallied round the Chartists, a movement which was to see its support swell at times of economic hardship. One such time was 1848, which saw republican uprisings in many European countries sparked by the successful February Revolution in France. King Louis Philippe was forced to abdicate and the Second Republic was established. In Britain the Chartists raised a national petition, rejected by Parliament, which was followed by disturbances throughout the rest of the year in some parts of the country, notably the north of England and London.

It was against this background that considerable social legislation was passed in Britain, aimed at improving the lot of the working people and blunting their anger. The 1844 and '47 Factory Acts are discussed in the next chapter. One of the Acts which had an important and direct impact on Linlithgow was the Burgh Trading Act. The historic rights of many burghs to control the commerce that took place within them had been conceived as a way of nurturing and encouraging trade but had come to act as a restriction. In 1901 a journalist wrote in the Linlithgowshire Gazette:

> 'Such has been the speed of modern progress and so complete the severance from old ties, that it is now hard to realise it was only in 1846 the Burgh Trading Act was passed, which enabled any person to carry on or exercise any trade or handicraft in any Burgh or elsewhere in Scotland, without being a Burgess of the Burgh, or a Guild Brother, or a member of any Guild, Craft, or Incorporation. Trade, at one time nurtured by the exclusive privileges possessed by the Free Burghs, came eventually to be stifled by them.'[65]

By 1851 it is clear that the Act had been effective within Linlithgow with traders, merchants and craftsmen from many parts of the country operating in the town.

Though there was no revolution in Scotland in 1848, local government was very aware of the need to alleviate the worst of the suffering caused by the economic downturn, especially given its new responsibilities for poor relief. In Linlithgow,

---

65   *Linlithgowshire Gazette, 26th April 1901, p6*

the Council took on 30 unemployed men in a public works programme to reclaim 'a piece of wild ground at the eastern extremity of the burgh'.[66]

Over the next two years conditions improved, order was restored across Europe, and the ruling classes began to breathe more easily.

---

66   *Ibid.*

CHAPTER TWO
THE BROADER
CONTEXT

The Wider World

Improvements in transport and communication continued to make the world a smaller place, as illustrated by two events in 1850. On 28th February the 'City of Glasgow' was launched. She was 'the first ship intended to open up steam communication between Glasgow and New York.'[69] This ship was to run a regular service of six two month long trips across the Atlantic and back. The second event was the laying of the first submarine telegraph cable, between Britain and France.

The British Prime Minister had been Lord John Russell since 1846, when Peel had resigned after repealing the Corn Laws. Russell was the last 'Whig' Prime Minister – after losing power in 1852 the party returned to power as the Liberal Party in 1855. The events which precipitated the fall of his government had their roots in 1851. Louis Napoleon overthrew the French constitution and declared himself Emperor Napoleon III. Without authorisation from Russell (but egged on by Queen Victoria) the Foreign Secretary, Lord Palmerston, backed Napoleon. Palmerston was dismissed and the subsequent recrimination brought the administration to an end. By the end of the year, 1852 was to see three Prime Ministers with the Earl of Derby's short-lived government succeeded by that of the Earl of Aberdeen.

In London, Prince Albert's brainchild, the Great Exhibition, was visited by 6.2 million people who saw 13,000 exhibits. It was a showcase for many advances which were changing the face of industry and agriculture.

In the USA the little remembered Millard Fillmore was President and the hot topic was slavery. Isaac Singer invented the single-thread domestic sewing machine and Herman Melville published Moby Dick.

Britain had become the dominant industrial power in the world economy. Initial success through textiles was being built on by the rapid spread of the railways and the innovative use of steam power and steel.

The Local Picture

With Westminster politics on the bubble this was a very interesting time for Linlithgow to take centre stage in national politics, at least for a few weeks.

69   *Glasgow Herald, Friday 1st March 1850*

It is tempting to say that by-election fever gripped the town in late January and February 1851. Certainly it was an ill-tempered affair and the result did not go the way the people, or at least the voters, of Linlithgow, wished.

Together, Linlithgow, Falkirk, Airdrie, Hamilton and Lanark formed a constituency called the Falkirk District of Burghs. It had a long history of unsatisfactory elections. In 1841 William Baird, an iron-works owner in Airdrie, had won the seat amidst accusations of malpractice in his home town. A by-election in 1846 between Lord Lincoln and Mr Wilson saw: 'The malpractices confined previously to Airdrie, extended to the other burghs.'[70] Worse was to follow in the general election of 1847, when Lord Lincoln faced Mr Boyd: 'The scenes of dissipation, treating, and corruption became almost as bad at Falkirk and Hamilton as they had been in Airdrie.'[71]

In 1851 this contentious seat was to be subject to another by-election. Two candidates came forward: George Loch of Glasgow, who supported the government, and was thus a Liberal, and William Baird's brother James Baird. Like William, James was an iron-works owner in Airdrie and a Conservative. Loch and Baird both campaigned on a platform that would be familiar to modern politicians: promoting business and eliminating waste and inefficiency. Both attended public meetings in all five burghs. An account in the Scotsman of the hustings in Falkirk, stated that Mr Loch was supported by Mr Dawson, Provost Hardy and various magistrates and councillors of Linlithgow. Over 3,000 people attended 'who, on the whole, conducted themselves with great propriety...and entered apparently with much zest into the personal bickerings that occurred between the candidates and their more prominent supporters.'[72]

Linlithgow's Mr John Dawson seconded the motion to adopt Mr Loch, commending him as a free-trader. He added, 'The electors must act independently; they must not get carried away with drink.'[73] These were to prove to be prophetic words.

Mr Baird emphasised his local connections in comparison to Mr Loch, whose day job was factor to the Duke of Sutherland. Mr Baird attacked Mr Loch for his involvement in the Highland clearances, showing that this was an issue which lowland Scots were already aware of. This may have played especially well in

---

70   Caledonian Mercury, 8th May 1851
71   Caledonian Mercury, 8th May 1851
72   The Scotsman, 12th February 1851
73   The Scotsman, 12th February 1851

Linlithgow where, in January 1847, the great and the good of the county had gathered at a public meeting to raise funds for the relief of destitute people in the Highlands and Islands. This had raised an impressive sum just short of £370.[74]

Both candidates wrote to the press that they had endeavoured, as far as possible to visit every voter.[75] Despite the extension of the franchise in the 1832 Reform Act the number of men (no women) who had the franchise was still pretty low, making this not as impractical as it may sound. This can be seen from the electoral returns:

	Mr Loch	Mr Baird
Falkirk	168	114
Linlithgow	45	33
Airdrie	127	280
Hamilton	133	75
Lanark	71	97
Total	544	599

Despite the support of Falkirk, Linlithgow and Hamilton, Mr Loch lost by 55 votes. The results were announced in Falkirk at noon on Friday 14th February, the day after the election. This followed an evening of disorder in Airdrie, as reported in the Caledonian Mercury:

'After the conclusion of the poll, a riot of a somewhat serious description occurred at Airdrie. A mob assembled around Mr Baird's committee-rooms, and became violent and unruly. They were charged by a body of police, sent from Glasgow, who, however, were received with a furious discharge of offensive missiles, and in the melee several were injured. An additional detachment of police was sent out from Glasgow about six o'clock. They were followed at eight by a party of military, consisting of two companies of foot and one of dragoons. Sheriff Alison accompanied the latter body. Soon after their departure, a message was received that their presence at the scene would be unnecessary.'[76]

At the declaration Mr Baird was badly received by the crowd, Mr Loch, rapturously. In his acceptance speech Mr Baird took the opportunity to publicly

---

74   *Caledonian Mercury, 18th January 1847*
75   *Glasgow Herald, Friday 7th February 1851*
76   *Caledonian Mercury, Monday 17th February 1851*

deny Mr Loch's accusation that he was a breaker of the law. Mr Baird accused Mr Loch's agent and friends of 'carrying away voters by force' even from 'the very polling booth' and of casting votes in the names of dead people.

The fallout from this election reached as far as Westminster.[77] Accusations were made by no less a man than the great radical MP Richard Cobden that Mr Baird had bought the election by bribing voters with cash payments and by offering free drink in 41 public houses in Airdrie: children as young as eight were reported to have staggered home drunk. There were calls for a public inquiry into allegations of bribery and corruption but no action was taken.

The year 1851 marked an important point in the history of the governance of the burgh of Linlithgow: it was the last year in which the council retained its mediaeval form with representatives from the traditional trades.

It may either be said that the Council took a laudable interest in national affairs, or that they had too much time on their hands. They petitioned Parliament on a number of Bills and other political matters, making sure their approval or disapproval was noted. Amongst other things, they were for the abolition of income tax and the reduction in the duty on fire insurance but against the Prison Bill, the Education Bill and the Bill for the Better Regulation of Public-Houses. They also supported the bill which sought to trim the number of councillors and magistrates in certain royal burghs, one of which was of course Linlithgow. In its 1901 retrospective series 'Linlithgow in 1851' the Linlithgowshire Gazette wrote:

> 'A Council of 27 for such a small town as Linlithgow was distinctly overweighted, and the Council showed its wisdom, or its weariness, in petitioning in favour of the bill, which reduced the number to 15.'[78]

It seems to have been a wet winter. In January the council discussed unusually high water levels in the loch which obstructed the sewers and damaged lochside gardens. The next month there were concerns about the damage done to the parapet wall of Avonbridge after continued flooding of the river.

The railway toll case, mentioned by Andrew Bell, was still progressing eight years on. In March 1851 it came before the House of Lords. On the fourth day the Lord Chancellor had to ask where any books on Scots Law could be found.[79]

---

77   *Hansard, 6th May 1851*
78   *Linlithgowshire Gazette, 12th April 1901, p6*
79   *The Scotsman, 22nd March 1851*

Had it only just occurred to him this might be useful? The on-going cost of the action was a concern to the council and in May Provost Hardy sought out financial assistance at the Convention of Royal Burghs, arguing that 'it was a case which had important bearing on the rights and privileges of all the burghs of Scotland.'[80] Mr Roberts, from Selkirk, replied that he 'did not think that the burgh of Linlithgow deserved any sympathy at all in the matter, as they were seeking, at the expense of the shareholders of the Edinburgh and Glasgow Railway, to get a large sum of money in the shape of customs dues for which they gave no equivalent.'[81] The Convention resolved not to interfere.

The Riding of the Marches took place on Tuesday 17th June after which the Council treated itself to a meal at the Star and Garter. To be fair, their bill only came to ten shillings, or less than two pence a head in decimal currency. In comparison the expenses for music that day came to £1 1s.

Earlier that week, the town had turned out in large numbers for an event held in the nave of St Michael's, described in detail in an article in the Scotsman on the importance of encouraging musical taste.[82] Praising the meeting it recorded that:

> 'From 16 to 20 young people of the Established Church there have for some time, with the countenance and approval of the Rev. Dr Bell, and under the gratuitous instruction of Mr Ellison, the keeper of the prison, devoted some of their leisure hours to the practice of Church music...'

> 'A respected family in the neighbourhood offered the aid of a valuable harmonium, an instrument analogous to the organ, and other instruments, and they and Mr C.W. Müller kindly gave their assistance as performers. Everything was arranged in a quiet unostentatious manner. The admission was a penny, merely to cover expenses. About three or four hundred persons attended, of all persuasions and classes. The effect of the various tunes, pieces, etc, sounding through the noble old edifice, was surprisingly beautiful, and the selection and performance both of some of the fine old tunes and of some more modern music of the great masters, adapted to the psalms, paraphrases, doxologies, etc, was admirable. After the choral performance, a few fine solemn airs were beautifully played on the harmonium. The whole was concluded with God Save the Queen, in which the choir and many of the audience joined. Much gratification was expressed by all present, and many observed that their prejudices against

80   Glasgow Herald, 18th May 1851
81   Glasgow Herald, 18th May 1851
82   The Scotsman, 14th June 1851

instrumental accompaniment were greatly shaken or entirely removed by this experiment."

Presbyterians didn't hold with musical accompaniment in church. Perhaps this event helped to change their views. The church was, of course, to become established as one of the foremost venues in the locality for musical performances – a position it holds to this day.

The big event in July was the Kinneil Races. John Hardy, the Provost of Linlithgow, acted as secretary, taking entries in the Star and Garter on the afternoon of Wednesday 9th.[83] Two days later many townspeople set out to enjoy an eight race card. The Caledonian Mercury reported that:

> *'These races took place on Friday in the large park at Kinneil, near Bo'ness, in the grounds of Mr Wilson of Dundyvan, used annually for the last five years as the race-course. A great crowd of spectators was collected from Linlithgow, Bo'ness, Grangemouth, Falkirk and neighbourhood; and the races were of a more successful character than hitherto.'* [84]

Journalists reported great excitement along the route of the royal train journey to and from Balmoral. On Friday 29th August the train pulled into Linlithgow Station 'at 8.52 for a few seconds to take in water.'[85] The Morning Chronicle described 'enthusiastic cheering from the assembled crowds'[86] at a number of Scottish towns including Linlithgow.

On Tuesdsay 7th October the royal party departed Balmoral Station at exactly 8am on its way to Edinburgh. As it passed though Linlithgow at 6.13pm that evening it 'slowed to some extent out of deference to the inhabitants of that ancient regal seat, who were not one whit behind any of the other places to which we have adverted in their expressions of loyalty.'[87]

After the flooding in January and February, the year also finished with a blast of winter. By early December the loch was frozen, allowing the curling season to commence. On Thursday 4th December, after three hours of play, Linlithgow Juniors defeated Camelon Club by three shots to win the district medal awarded

---

83   *Glasgow Herald, 23rd June 1851*
84   *Caledonian Mercury, 14th July 1851*
85   *Caledonian Mercury, 1st September 1851*
86   *The Morning Chronicle, 30th August 1851*
87   *Glasgow Herald, 10th October 1851*

by the Royal Caledonian Curling Club.[88] The Scotsman tells us, in a match report published on the 6th of December, that John McElfrish, whom we will meet again later as a glue maker, was a successful curler.[89] On the tenth of December the same paper reported a violent storm:

> *'In Linlithgow, on Monday morning, a large currying shed, upwards of 100 feet in length, was unroofed at one fell swoop while the workmen were employed below. A large portion of an old house was also blown in while the inmates were in bed. They were extricated with some difficulty. The venerable willow which adorned the islet in the Loch, and which has withstood the storm for ages, has at last been laid low.'* [90]

It went on to note that a chimney-stalk at Messers Dawson's milling establishment at Bonnytoun was thrown down.

It had been a year in which Linlithgow had made cameo appearances on the national stage though the rhythm of life had continued in its normal pattern to its established calendar. It marked the end of the town council in its traditional format and saw the venerable willow laid low, but the Marches was held on the first Tuesday after the second Thursday in June and the weather gave everyone plenty to talk about.

The 1851 Census – A Moment In Time

The 1851 census was held on the night of the 30th of March, and we are indebted to those who undertook the work for the picture we have of the population of the parish. Much of the remainder of this book rests upon an analysis of the data gathered that night. It is very much a snapshot in time: a census taken later in the year, at harvest time for example, would have provided different results. Furthermore, the census does not tell us about people who were out of the area on 30th March. Acknowledging these limitations, what the census does do is provide us with a picture of Linlithgow in greater detail than any single source prior to that date. It provides reliable data from which we can gain a good understanding of the state of the parish and its industries, especially when put in context by the other sources available to us.

---

88 *Caledonian Mercury, 8th December 1851*
89 *The Scotsman, 6th December 1851*
90 *The Scotsman, 10th December 1851*

Having raised the question of people who were absent, it is worth examining the obverse side of the coin: by looking at the census records for people who were visitors to the town we can form an idea of the number of residents who were likely to be elsewhere. Across the parish there are only a total of 87 individuals recorded in this way and it is clear that a significant number of these were in fact working in the vicinity: they were staying in somebody else's home (perhaps until they could sort out accommodation), rather than visiting in the sense of taking a holiday. Nearly a quarter (20) were from Linlithgow itself, of whom four are recorded as working at the calico print works. The Irish made up the largest contingent of 'visitors' with 22. The men are recorded as railway or agricultural labourers, miners or hawkers. All of these professions had mobile workforces and it seems most likely that these men, some with their wives and children, were either working, or seeking work, locally. On the other hand, a few people can be identified as visitors in the leisure sense. For example, two English young ladies, Sarah and Harriet Whinney, were staying with the distillery owning Dawsons of Green Park. In many cases the evidence simply does not exist to allow a conclusion to be reached on the nature of the 'visit'. However, there is no reason to believe that a significant number of people were on leisure visits, or passing through, on the night of the 30th March, and thus no reason to believe that a significant number of people were absent.

a.   Population – A Summary

To start with, some bald figures. The population of the parish of Linlithgow in 1851 was recorded as being 6,115. This represented an increase of 165 from 1841, a time at which we know from the New Statistical Account the population was considered to be inflated by the number of labourers present due to the construction of the railway. Table 2 shows how the population had grown since the inception of national censuses in 1801.

Table 2 shows that the proportion of residents of the parish who lived within the burgh had increased slightly over the first half of the nineteenth century. This would no doubt have been more pronounced had Linlithgow Bridge been included within the burgh. We have seen that industry had developed along the Avon and the west end of the loch and many of the workers lived in, or moved to, the village. The 1851 census was the first in which the number of people outwith the burgh actually fell.

Table 2. Population figures for Linlithgow from census returns

	Parish	Town	Country	%-age in Burgh
1801	3,594			
1811	4,022	2,557	1,465	63.6%
1821	4,692	3,112	1,580	66.3%
1831	4,874	3,187	1,687	65.4%
1841	5,950	3,872	2,078	65.1%
1851	6,115	4,071	2,044	66.6%

Just over half of the population of the parish, 3211, had been born there. A further 648 had moved in from other parts of West Lothian. The largest numbers had come from:

- Bo'ness   121
- Kirkliston   83
- Torphichen   80
- Bathgate   75
- Abercorn   62

There are no big surprises in this list as these are all close to Linlithgow, and Bo'ness was the second most populous parish in the county behind Linlithgow, ahead of third placed Bathgate. At this time, Livingston parish had one of the smallest populations, although that was to change over the remainder of the decade. Interestingly, in terms of parishes the one which contributed the second greatest number of people to Linlithgow's population was not actually within West Lothian. A total of 94 of the residents had been born in Muiravonside which, though in Stirlingshire, was of course adjacent to Linlithgow parish.

Outnumbering incomers from the rest of the county was the Irish contingent of 713. Next came the neighbouring counties:

- Midlothian   410
- Stirlingshire   316 (including the 94 from Muiravonside)
- Lanarkshire   166

Perthshire contributed 75 people and Fife 70. From there on the numbers decline rapidly, though the parish had representatives from every county in Scotland apart from Orkney and Shetland. 67 English born people lived in the parish. Though there were no Welsh, there were two Americans, two Canadians, and one person each born in France, Italy and the East Indies!

A full breakdown of the population by place of birth can be found in Tables 17, 18 and 19 in the Appendix.

Women slightly outnumbered men. There were 96.3 men for every 100 women. Though unremarkable on the face of it, this does in fact make Linlithgow quite unusual. In the Eastern Lowlands the average was 89.9 men for every 100 women and across Scotland as a whole 92.8. This puts Linlithgow not just above the Scottish average but also above that for England and Wales, which was 96.0.[91] A steadily increasing population, with a good balance of men to women, suggests that Linlithgow was an attractive place to live, doing relatively well at holding on to its men at a time when many other places were losing a significant proportion of them.

When examining the ages given, it is very noticeable that there are large spikes at round numbers and troughs on either side. It may be supposed that some people considered themselves to be, say, about 40 and either were not entirely sure or saw no reason to be more accurate. This is illustrated in Figure 2. Nowadays we might expect the peaks to be in the numbers ending in nine rather than zero.

As would be expected, the high majority of the young people in the parish had been born there. This is illustrated in Figure 3, which splits residents into those born in Linlithgow, those who had come in from other parts of West Lothian and those who came from further afield. Due to the peaks and troughs in the ages shown in Figure 2 the ages have been rolled up into five-year bands. Up to the 15-19 age group a resident of the parish was far more likely to be a native, but from 20-24 up to 50-54 they were most likely to have come in from outside West Lothian. While the census does not inform us when individuals moved to the parish it is interesting to note that people in this higher age group would have been in their early twenties when the canal was opened: an event which brought the rest of the country closer. Even in the mid nineteenth century, Linlithgow was a town of incomers. The peak age group for residents who had come from another part of West Lothian was 14-19. This will be discussed later.

Effectively, the upper end of the age range was 87. I say 'effectively' because the town was home to the remarkable John Campbell from Morven, Argyll: 106 years old and apparently still working as a general labourer. Not only that but he and his 55 year old wife had children aged 7 and 10! John's great age can be verified to an extent in that in the 1841 census he gave his age as 96. Trailing far behind

91   Flinn, p317 (all figures)

him, there were four people who gave their age as 87, just ahead of three 86 year olds. The 87 year olds comprised David Laurie from Ratho (agricultural labourer and pauper), Mary Flin from Ireland (beggar), Alexander Yorkston from Dunbar (military pensioner) and Alexander Hardie from Carriden (retired farmer). With no welfare state at this time, retirement was only an option for a lucky few.

There would not appear from this data to be any significant differences between the sexes, although women are more common amongst those people who were 60 years plus (see Figure 4), outnumbering the men by about 4:3.

In the 1841 Census, Baillie found a large jump in the male population in the 20-24 age group[92] which would seem likely to have been caused by railway labourers. In 1851 there is no equivalent spike at 30-34 confirming that many of these people had moved on. Overall, the decrease in population against age appears to be quite steady.

---

92   *Baillie, p47*

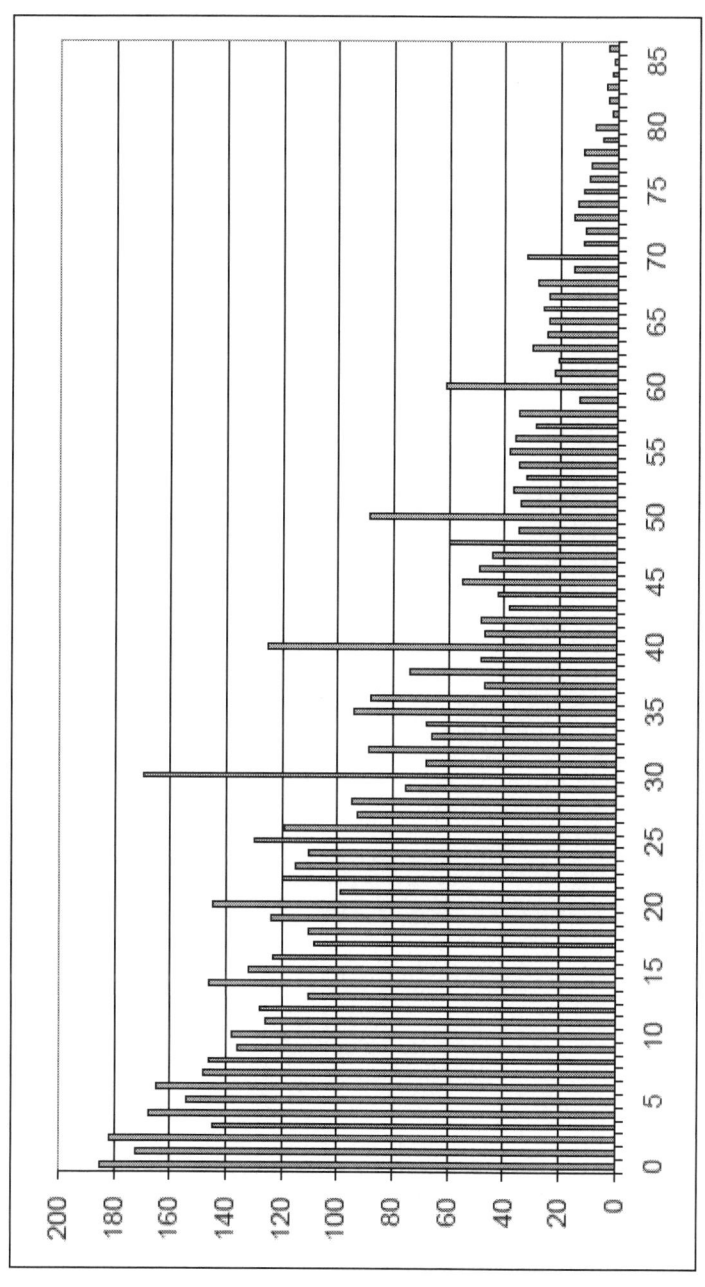

Figure 2: Population of Linlithgow by age

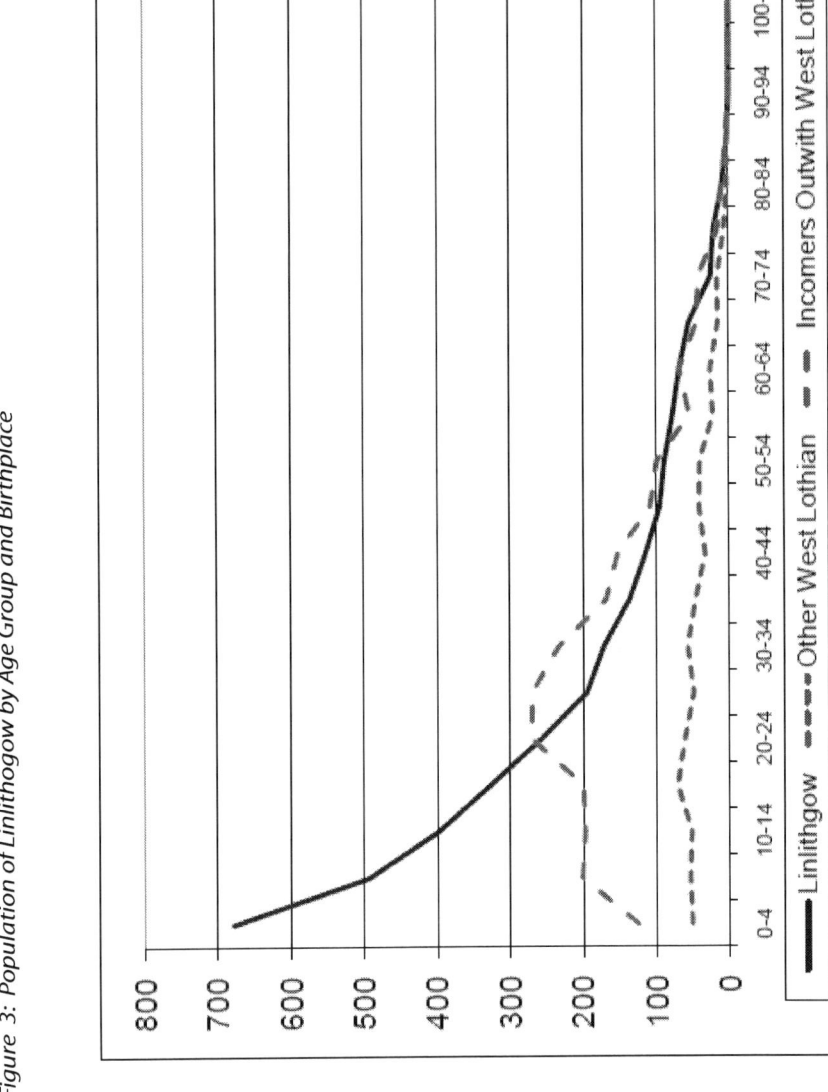

Figure 3: Population of Linlithgow by Age Group and Birthplace

Figure 4: Male and Female Population by Age Groups

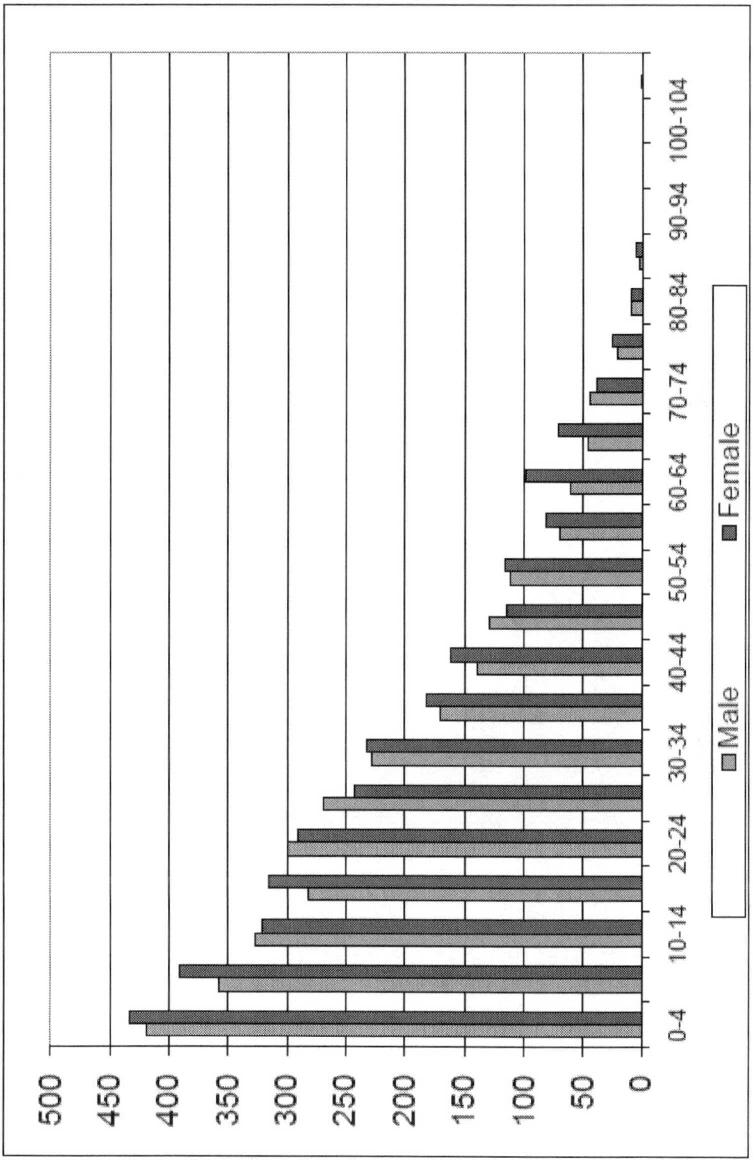

b.   The Physical Growth of Linlithgow

The town was mapped in 1820 by John Wood and then again in 1856 by the Ordnance Survey. The latter formed part of the first national mapping of Britain. From the census data we know that the population of Linlithgow burgh had grown by about a third from 1821 to 1851 and was then to decline slightly by 1861. This suggests that the bulk of the changes between the two maps are likely to have been made by 1851.

As we can see in Wood's map (on page 25), the town was very much one street running from the West Port to what is now the Star & Garter, where it split into the High and Low Ports, quickly petering out thereafter. Other than that, there is little more to the town than a few buildings to the south, between the High Street and the canal.

In the Ordnance Survey first edition map we see that the western edge of the town remained largely unchanged, probably because it was hard up against the burgh boundary. To the east, there had been minor growth along the Low and High Ports. The St Magdalene's Distillery marked the new limit of the town in that direction. The big change from 1820 was of course the railway, which cut through land that in Wood's map was largely unoccupied. Along with the railway, we see that two roads had been created running along each side of it. The Royal Terrace/Strawberry Bank area was becoming built up in what appears to be a piecemeal fashion. We see new buildings in a number of the wynds that linked the High Street to the new roads, in particular along New Well Wynd and Lion Well Wynd.

Across the canal, Victoria Place has been built and Friarbank House, Clarendon House and Rivalds Green can be seen down what would become Manse Road and Friars' Brae.

As well as the development of new areas, a number of new buildings had been constructed within the historic core of the burgh, many of which still survive. Listed building descriptions published by Historic Scotland indicate that, in particular, a number of new buildings were built in the west end of the south side of the High Street in the mid nineteenth century. Examples are numbers 167 to 171 (Linlithgow DIY and Flowers by Carolyn at the time of writing) and 213 to 221 (W L Morrison and the British Red Cross).

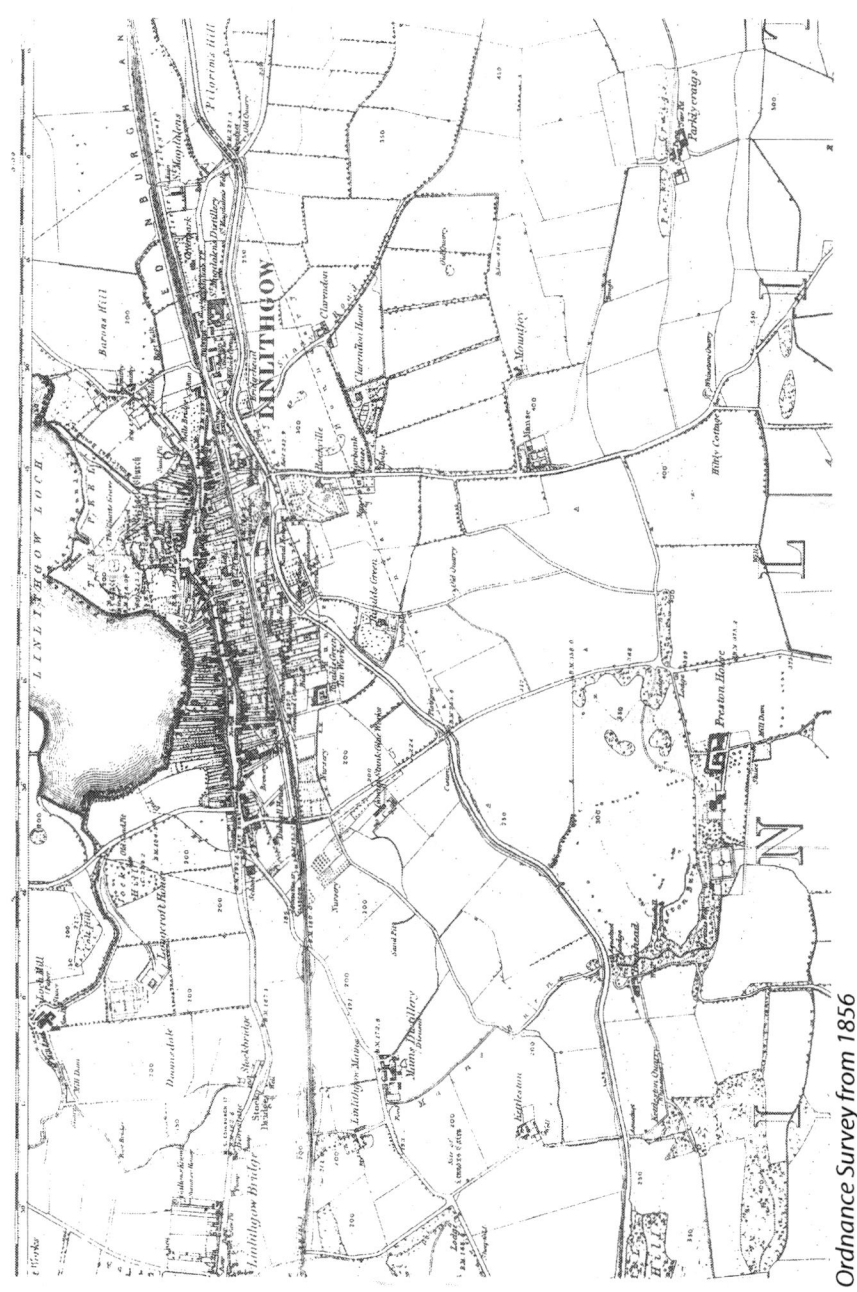

Ordnance Survey from 1856
Reproduced by permission of the Trustees of the National Library of Scotland

Outwith the town, we can see a number of the manufacturing enterprises that employed people from the town. The map shows the Loch Mill (paper mill) to the north-west. To the south are the Gowan Stank Glue Works and Rivalds Green Tan Works.

c.   Children

Linlithgow in 1851 was a town with a young population: the average age was 25, the median age was 21, and just over a third of the population were aged thirteen or younger. The division between childhood and adulthood was very unclear and to an extent depended on how well off the child's parents were. This was a time before the universal provision of education, but it was the norm for most children to have around six or seven years at school.[93] There was no formal starting age.

---

93   *School attendance was not compulsory until the 1872 Education Act and even then there were ways round it for those who were determined.*

217-221 High Street
In 1851 217 was home to the Potters (baker), the Kerrs (shoemaker) and the Andersons (tanner). 221 was home to two families of Aikenheads (both shoemakers), Elizabeth Wardrop (a house proprietrix) and the Robertsons (leather dresser).

100 High Street (unrendered building in the middle)
In 1851 the building was home to 25 people across six families:
- nailer John Rae and his wife Janet
- Mary Ann Robertson, her husband (a calico printer who was not present that night) and their four children
- shoemaker William Calder and his three sons,
- another shoemaker, William Grandison, his wife Elizabeth and their two daughters
- Ann Regan, her husband (a rag store keeper, absent, like Mr Robertson above), their five children and a grandson
- Margaret Dodds and her son William, a shoemaker, and their lodger David Robertson (gardener)

The youngest children to be described in the census as scholars are three two year old boys. Similarly, there was no minimum age for starting to work. Through the nineteenth century a series of Acts sought to improve the working conditions of children and women. The 1819 Factory Act had forbidden children under nine to work in cotton mills. The 1842 Mines Act banned the use of women and young children underground. The Factory Acts of 1844 and 1847 had reduced the working day for those aged nine to thirteen to six and a half hours, and for women and young persons aged fourteen to eighteen to just ten hours. The 1850 Factory Act set out to control the times of day in which the hours could be worked and enshrined Saturday afternoon as time off. Unfortunately, poor drafting of the laws meant that employers found ways round the good intent of the lawmakers. It was not until later in the century that many of the prevalent evils were eliminated.[94] In practice, the children of Linlithgow begin to have an occupation recorded against them from the age of seven. It isn't until we look at children aged twelve that we start to see significant numbers who are working. Some children were not recorded in the census either as scholars or as working. In the Occupation field in the census they were often described as 'At Home', by their relationship to the head of the household (e.g., 'Daughter of labourer'), or the field was simply left blank.

The pattern of school attendance was broadly similar for girls and boys, though there are some differences. Boys began to attend school in significant numbers from age five, while for girls it was age six. Most boys aged twelve were still at school, while a slim majority of girls had left at that age. For the purposes of this work we will take the core school period to be five to twelve. Table 20 and Figures 5 and 6 (all in the Appendix) show the numbers and percentages of children at school or in formal work by sex and age.

For both boys and girls, the numbers in work overtake the number in school at age thirteen. The percentage of boys in formal employment rises rapidly into the 80 and 90 percents. For girls the numbers rise more slowly and no higher than 80%. This suggests that up to 20% of girls in their mid teens had left school and were working informally at home or in the family business.

In 1843, Andrew Bell recorded that 'In 1834, there were 547 children attending all the schools in the parish, and since then the number has not decreased.'[95] While this does not give us fixed data for his period, it does give us two points for comparison nine years apart. In 1851, we find an increase of more than two

---

94   *Gardiner & Wenborn, p737*
95   *NSA, p185*

thirds to 923. Given that the total population had increased by around a fifth, this is a hugely disproportionate rise: since there is no evidence of a baby boom, it may suggest that participation levels had gone up, perhaps explained in part by the greater proportion living in the town rather than the countryside.

This photograph of the Cross Well was taken by Thomas Begbie in the 1850s or 1860s. Two little girls in the bottom right hand corner seem to have struggled to sit still for the length of the exposure.

Table 3. Children at School Aged 5-12 by place of birth

Place of Birth	% Boys at School	% Girls at School
Linlithgow & West Lothian	79	71
Midlothian, Stirlingshire & Lanarkshire	69	73
Other Scottish Counties	68	68
Ireland	16	24

The place of birth of the children provides further insights. Taking the school period to be ages five to twelve (shown highlighted in Table 20, Appendix), gives a school-age population of 1138 (of whom 775 were recorded as scholars). A high majority of these children (735 of the 1138) were born in Linlithgow parish. With 100 school-age children, the next largest group came not from West Lothian or the neighbouring counties, but Ireland. A further 78 came from other parts of West Lothian. The Neighbouring counties to West Lothian, Midlothian, Stirlingshire and Lanarkshire, made up the next largest group in this age group followed by small numbers from other Scottish counties.

Table 3 shows that the big story as regards schooling was the very low participation rate of the Irish. This will be discussed in the section on the Irish. As for the rest, the schooling figure for locally born boys is notably higher than for other areas. For girls the figures are less clear cut.

d.   Those Not in Formal Employment

The Census tells us a great deal of information about the parish by recording the jobs people did. However, a substantial section of the population was not in formal employment. Given that most people were working by the time they were thirteen, for the purposes of this study, 'adult' is used to cover people from that age onwards.

Table 4. Adults (13+) Not In Formal Employment

	Male	Female	Total
No Employment Given	37	892	925
Independently Wealthy	15	29	44
Relations	16	145	161
Pauper	18	67	85
Scholars	52	51	103

In total, these categories cover 7% of men and 55% of women in the parish.

Most to be envied were those who were in some way independently wealthy. This category included people described as annuitants, stockholders, gentlewomen and pensioners of various descriptions. There were fifteen men and 29 women in this category. Helen Baird, 63, of 5 The Cross, is described simply as being a 'possessor of money'.

The largest group of those not formally employed were women. The main sources of employment open to women were low status. If a household could afford for the wife not to have a job then they generally didn't work. A total of 952 (almost 45%) of the women of the parish were not so fortunate and have an occupation recorded against them. Given large family sizes and the absence of modern appliances, being a housewife was by no means an easy option: slightly better off households would employ one or more servants.

A handful of men (37) have no occupation or source of income recorded against them: most of them were over 60, although James Morgan, 38, from Ireland was described as being in 'delicate health'.

A number of adults (i.e., aged thirteen or over) were described in terms of their relationship to the head of the house. This category includes sixteen men and 145 women. Where the head of the house was a businessman of some sort it seems probable that the relation was working as part of the business. This is most likely to hold true in agriculture. For example, ten of the men are farmers' sons, living on the farm and may be supposed to be working for their fathers. The same is likely to be true of most of the 31 daughters, wives and other female relations of farmers and the nineteen female relations of farm servants or agricultural labourers. It may also be the case with some of the other 'sons'. However, in the majority of cases this seems tenuous and the 'relation' probably had no involvement in the head's occupation. For example, eleven women were described by their relationship to railway labourers. A daughter of a minister was certainly not a de facto minister and a wife of a railway policeman would not have had any significant role is his work. Sometimes the relationship goes through a second person. It is hard to tell anything about the occupation of someone who was listed as 'Wife's Aunt'!

The scholars require no explanation. Table 20 and Figures 5 and 6 (all in the Appendix) give further information on them.

Finally, there are a group of people who were unable to support themselves - the paupers and beggars. The number of people in this category could be used as an indicator for the general health of the economy. On the 27th February 1850 the Aberdeen Journal covered the annual report by the Board of Supervision for the relief of the poor in Scotland to both houses of parliament. They divided the poor into two groups, which the census does not allow us to do – registered and casual. The former were long-term poor while the latter dipped in and out of poverty. Though the number of registered poor had increased slightly, they were happy to report that:

> 'The number of casual poor has been a good deal diminished, a circumstance that speaks favourably of the prosperity of the manufacturing interests, for we fear that the diminution has not extended to the rural districts in these times of severe agricultural depression.'[96]

This report was for the year 1849. Looking at the figures reported in the 1850, 1851 and 1852 reports[97] (each for the previous year) we find:

Table 5. Changes in the numbers of poor in Linlithgow and Scotland, 1849-51

Year	West Lothian (Linlithgowshire) Poor				Scotland Poor			
	Registered	Change	Casual	Change	Registered	Change	Casual	Change
1849	818		1050		106,434		95,686	
1850	906	+11%	828	-21%	101,454	-5%	53,070	-45%
1851	987	+9%	653	-21%	99,777	-2%	42,093	-21%

---

96   *The Aberdeen Journal, Wednesday 27th February 1850*
97   *The Aberdeen Journal, Wednesday 27th February 1850, Wednesday 19th February 1851 & Wednesday 25th February 1852*

The number of registered poor in the county was rising at a time when it was falling nationally. The number of casual poor in the county was decreasing but not as impressively as at national level. This indicates that West Lothian as a whole was not experiencing improved economic conditions to the same extent as the rest of the country.

It is not possible to drill down to identify variations between the different parishes within the county. What we can see from the 1851 census is that across the county 430 people are recorded as either 'pauper', 'beggar' or 'receiving parish relief' (from now on grouped together as paupers). The Board of Supervision reported 987 registered poor in the county at this time, which seems to leave a gap of 557 poor people unaccounted for in the census. The census figure does not include dependents, which may account for some of the difference, or perhaps the Board had a more liberal definition of the poor. A further factor may have been a reluctance on the part of paupers to identify themselves as such to the census enumerators. In any case, the figure of 430 from the census can be split into 85 within Linlithgow parish and 345 in the other parishes. Taking these as a proportion of the relative populations this would mean one pauper for every 72.0 people in Linlithgow against one pauper for every 70.6 in other parishes. Linlithgow parish may have had slightly fewer paupers than the rest of the county but if so the difference was probably difficult to notice.

Linlithgow's 85 were eighteen men and 67 women paupers. Most of these were over 50 years old. Many have a dual designation such as Pauper Washerwoman, giving an occupation that was either insufficiently lucrative to support them or which they were no longer able to undertake. In this group we find a quarter of the tambourers whose desperate condition Andrew Bell had described in 1843.

CHAPTER THREE
EMPLOYMENT

This chapter analyses the different areas of employment in Linlithgow in 1851, with similar occupations grouped together.

Each occupation or industry is analysed using comparable figures, where they are available, from the 1841 census, the 1843 Statistical Account, and the two trade directories, to try to establish whether the numbers involved were increasing, decreasing or stable. An analysis is done to identify the age and place of birth profiles of each workforce in order to understand which occupations attracted people at different stages of life and from which part of the country, which had aging workers and which were taking on apprentices. Large analytical sections are followed by short summary sections, covering the main findings.

We will start with a summary of the main areas of employment and trends. Following that, there are a series of sections giving a more detailed analysis of each individual area. In the following chapter there is an analysis of the types of employment undertaken by place of birth.

Employment Summary

In 1851, the employment roles open to men and women were clearly differentiated. Even in the industries which had a mix of the sexes the roles taken rarely overlapped. Another great difference between the sexes when it came to employment was that 93% of men worked, or at least stated some form of employment, while only 45% of women did. To put it simply, a man was expected to work if he could while, as already discussed, a woman was expected not to work if she could afford it.

The figures in Table 6 are for people who had explicitly stated an occupation, as almost all men and about half of the women had done. As discussed in the preceding chapter there are insurmountable difficulties in accurately quantifying the informal efforts of other members of society. This is a particular problem for agriculture, as will be discussed later in this chapter.

Table 6. Top 5 Employment areas in Linlithgow, 1851

	Male		Female		Combined	
1	Agriculture	384	Servants	436	Agriculture	484
2	Shoemaking	326	Agriculture	100	Servants	456
3	Railways	270	Calico Printing	90	Shoemaking	340
4	General Labouring	94	Dressmaking	49	Railways	270
5	Calico Printing	64	Tambouring	48	Calico Printing	154

Table 6 shows us that many of the traditional employment areas were still going strong in 1851. Amongst men, agriculture remained the dominant sector across the rural parts of the parish while shoemaking dominated the town. The big contrast between these two sectors is that over three quarters of those involved in shoemaking were born in the parish while only just over one third of those involved in agriculture were natives. Shoemaking, of course, required a long apprenticeship leading to a well paid career while agriculture, the Agricultural Revolution notwithstanding, was dominated by low skilled labouring. The agricultural labour market was very mobile giving much greater opportunity, or creating a necessity, for incomers to make a new start away from their place of birth. We will see that this was one of the parts of the economy that saw a large number of incomers.

Currying and tanning continued to exist alongside shoemaking. Tanning appears to have been going into decline, with numbers falling and the average age rising due to competition from large manufacturers outside the county. Currying seems to have been unaffected at this stage.

One of the big changes since 1841 is the increase in the number of servants, suggesting increasing affluence amongst the middle ranks of the town, the skilled artisans and small business people. Like agriculture, going into service often meant moving away from one's place of birth – in this case largely for women rather than men. Again, this could be seen as an opportunity or a necessity. Only a third of the servants in the parish were born there.

One of the most surprising figures in Table 6 is the number of people, predominantly Irish, who gave their employment as railway labourers. The railway had been completed nine years earlier. The presence of this number of people in Linlithgow suggests that considerable maintenance was required and that Linlithgow was used as a depot for the work on the line west of Edinburgh.

EMPLOYMENT

General labourers still made up an important part of the workforce. A total of 63 more specialised labourers worked in the small quarries and mines across the parish. Linlithgow was never to be a significant mining area, unlike the south of the county, which would see an explosion of shale mining from 1852 onwards.

Calico printing had been a major employer since the 1780s and continued to be so until 1860. In 1851 we find a mixed male and female workforce including many young people. The tambourers continued to decline and many of them had become paupers. Many of the younger women who might have become tambourers in earlier days had become dressmakers. Indeed the increasing numbers of people employed in providing goods and services for the populace is another indication of a broader wealth base within the town. Hat makers, tailors and drapers were thriving. Looking more widely, there were 44 people involved in baking, fifteen in fleshing, 68 in grocery, spirits and related food and drink and 44 in other retail activities. The range and choice of goods available in the town was probably greater than at any previous time.

The town had been expanding and new houses built in old streets so it is not surprising to find that building related trades made up a significant portion of the workforce. With 60 men, the masons almost make it into the 'top five' list of male occupations. Though a large group, this was a decrease of a third from 1841 when their services had been much in demand during the construction of the railway. Many seem to have moved on and the number still present seems to have discouraged younger men from trying to work their way up. Masons were therefore uncharacteristic of the building trades in having an older age profile and a majority of incomers. Working with them were 80 wrights, joiners, carpenters, plasterers, house painters, slaters and a plumber. These trades were dominated by locals.

Looking at the other industries, paper making continued and now employed 53 people. Brewing and distilling also continued but even combined employed relatively few people (30). In all three cases the bulk of the jobs were low skilled and the bulk of the employees were incomers.

Turning to the professions, as the county town, Linlithgow had the county court and prison as well as other administrative functions. This made it the legal centre of the county with half a dozen writers (solicitors) and supporting staff. In total 32 people worked in law related jobs, while fourteen worked as tax collectors in one form or another.

Including two student teachers, there were seventeen teachers in the parish. Given that there were 923 scholars class sizes must have been pretty high! There were ten people involved in healthcare and seven in religion.

In conclusion, the 1851 census presents a picture of a parish which, though reliant on its traditional industries, was diversifying and enjoying increased levels of prosperity: a parish that was attractive to incomers and which was successful in holding onto its own.

Shoemaking

Comparative Data for Shoemaking Businesses

Pigot's Trade Directory (1837)	16
Slater's Trade Directory (1852)	26

We have seen that throughout the period under study shoemaking had been considered the staple industry of the town. In 1851 we find it flourishing, dominating the town, and a close second to agriculture as the largest employer of men across the parish. Indeed when the related trades such as tanning, currying, glue making and saddle making are included, they comfortably exceed agriculture.

Baillie's analysis of the 1841 census found 287 people in the burgh involved in this field. In the 1851 census we find 340 (of which all but fourteen were men). This figure is for the whole parish so it is not possible to make a direct comparison with Baillie's figure. However, the vast majority of the shoemakers were found within the burgh, suggesting that there had been an increase in the number of people working in this trade over the intervening decade. The 1851 figure meant that one in six of the working men of the parish were cordiners.

Like Pigot's Trade Directory of 1837, Slater's Trade Directory of 1852 gives us information about main businesses and business people of the town. From that we can see that as well as the number of employees increasing, so had the number of employers, from sixteen in 1837 to 26 in 1852.

Shoemaking, like many of other trades, had its hierarchy. At the bottom were the apprentices. Once they had served their time, and proved their skill, they became journeymen. At the top of the heap were the master shoemakers, shoe merchants and shoe manufacturers.

Shoemaking lay at the heart of the community and the next generation was 80% Linlithgow born. Apprentices started young, and often in the family firm. While we find two boys as young as ten given as apprentices, most were aged thirteen to sixteen. Only one young man was an apprentice past eighteen. This was George Frater, a 21 year old who had come all the way from Redcastle in Ross & Cromarty and lived with his grandmother, 80 year old pauper Mary Innes. She came from Lochbroom parish, also in Ross & Cromarty. Indeed, he was not only unusual for the age at which he was still learning his trade but also in that as an incomer he was taken on as an apprentice at all. Pauper though she was, Mary Innes may have been well connected. Also living with her was Andrew Ross, another Redcastle born grandson, who was an apprentice currier.

Journeymen shoemakers were of course a little older: the youngest recorded was fourteen and the average age was 33. Linlithgow born men again dominated with over three quarters of journeymen being born in the parish. The success of the industry had attracted men from as far afield as Wigtownshire and Sutherland, and indeed from Ireland and England. These men from outwith the parish tended to be older and had an average age of 40.

Not surprisingly those at the top of the trade, the masters, merchants and manufacturers, tended to be older still. Although we find one twenty year old man, John Alison, giving his profession as Master Shoemaker, the average age for these men was 44. John may have been overstating his status as he does not appear in Slater's Trade Directory the following year, or he may have moved elsewhere. The natives had an iron grip on the upper echelons. Of the seventeen men at the top of this trade, sixteen were born in the town and the seventeenth had only migrated from Carriden.

A substantial minority of men are recorded simply as a shoemaker, or boot and shoemaker. Since their ages range from eleven to 74 they must encompass people from apprentice upwards. Again, virtually 80% come from Linlithgow.

Table 7. Shoemakers in Linlithgow by rank

	Number in 1851 census	Percentage born in Linlithgow
Master Shoemaker	13	92%
Merchant/Manufacturer	4	100%
Journeyman	179	77%
Apprentice	57	82%
Shoemaker	63	79%
Boot & Shoemaker	8	100%

As well as the men, fourteen women worked in shoemaking as boot binders. Once again this was primarily a local affair with eleven of them having been born in Linlithgow.

Summary

Shoemaking was very much in the grip of local men: especially at the top and bottom of the trade, the masters and the apprentices. The number of people working in shoemaking had increased by about 20% over the preceding ten years, cementing its place at the heart of the burgh's economy.

Trades Related to Shoemaking

As has already been noted, shoemaking did not exist in isolation from other trades. At this time, the shoemakers still appear to have used locally produced leather. We have seen that the related trades of tanner and currier had long existed side by side with the dominant trade. A tanner would take raw animal hides and convert them into leather. A currier would take the tanned leather and work and stretch it into a condition where it could be used for the manufacture of such items as shoes, gloves, harnessing or bookbinding. There were also other spin-off industries such as saddle making and glue making. The work of fleshers, or butchers, obviously had a relationship with these trades, but as they were more akin to other shopkeepers in the town such as bakers and grocers, they are considered under 'Commerce'.

There was considerable overlap between the trades and between tradesmen and retailers. Several men put down multiple trades in the census. Where someone put down 'Tanner and Leather Merchant' or 'Master Currier and Grocer' it can be assumed that there was a relationship between the different parts of their business. Where someone puts down their occupation as being, for instance, 'Glue Maker, Tanner and Currier', 'Tanner and Currier', or 'Tanner, Currier and Knife Maker' they are harder to categorise. For those at the top of their trades, Slater's 1852 trade directory has been used to try to identify which trade to count them under. For those lower down the spectrum, their principal trade has been taken to be the first named.

a. Tanning

Comparative data for tanning businesses

Pigot's Trade Directory (1837)	6
Andrew Bell (1843)	5
Slater's Trade Directory (1852)	4

Linlithgow had never been more than a local manufacturer of leather and the town's industry came under threat from larger scale producers in other parts of the country. John Butt wrote 'Tanning was universally a market-town industry in the eighteenth century; by 1850 Maybole, Edinburgh and the Bridgeton suburb of Glasgow dominated the industry.'[98] Gradually, the competitiveness of local tanneries across the country, such as those in Linlithgow, was eroded until they shut down. The decline in tanning in Linlithgow had led to the Fraternity of Tanners dissolving itself in June 1847, dividing its funds amongst its members.

In 1843 Andrew Bell had reported 33 tanners in the parish. In the 1851 census there are only twenty people who give their employment as tanning.

As well as the number of employees, the number of tanning businesses was shrinking, as can be seen in the table above. Tanning was increasingly an older man's occupation: there were only three apprentices in the 1851 census. Discounting these three, the average age of the tanners was over 45. Those still involved in the trade were mostly locals, making up sixteen (80%) of the twenty.

---

98   *Butt, p17*

b.   Currying

Comparative data for currying businesses

Pigot's Trade Directory (1837)	5
Slater's Trade Directory (1852)	13

Currying was a big employer in 1841 with 43 people: in 1851 we find exactly the same number. In contrast to tanning, currying seems to have been seen as a trade with a future: a quarter of the curriers were apprentices. The journeymen and master curriers were a younger group than their equivalents in tanning, almost ten years younger, with an average age of just under 36. As with shoemaking and tanning, currying was dominated by local families: 36 (84%) of the men in the trade were born in Linlithgow parish.

The increase in the number of currying businesses since 1837, when three of the five shared one surname (Callander), suggests that the average size of a currying business was much smaller at this stage.

c.   Glue Making

In 1837 the town is recorded as having two glue making businesses, one under the delightfully named John Buncle of Jinkabout. In 1852 there were three: John Buncle remained and there were two new businesses. Given the smell that was associated with glue making, it is interesting to note that the McElfrish brothers John (the successful curler), Andrew and James advertised their side line as soap perfumers. There is a strong chance that these men were related to John Buncle. They were probably his nephews, as their parents were Elizabeth Buncle and Andrew McElfrish and the birth records show that John Buncle had a sister called Elizabeth who would have been the right age. In 1852 the McElfrish brothers diversified further, obtaining an alcohol license.

Glue making was very much a growth industry at this time. By the 1851 census the number had grown to 23 from the three people found by Baillie in the 1841 census. Again, local people had taken the lion's share of the jobs. Only three of the individuals were not born in the parish. Mark Lothian was a gluework labourer from Tranent, while James and Agnes Cuddie had come from Falkirk and Bothkennar (both in Stirlingshire). They ran a multidisciplinary business: glue making, tanning and currying, employing 35 men. Strangely they do not appear in the 1852 Trade Directory under any of these categories or any other.

Glue making is the only one of the related leather industries which has people classified as labourers: in 1851 six men fell into this category. The other seventeen comprise three young boys who were apprentices, three young men who were journeymen and eleven who were glue makers or manufacturers.

Alexander Murray was a glue maker and church officer, showing the respectability of the trade.

d.   Saddlers

In 1837 Linlithgow had two saddlers, William Greenfield from Selkirk and William Sutherland from Dunfermline. They were still the only two saddlers in the 1852 trade directory, by which time they were aged 43 and 55 respectively. In the 1851 census we find nine people employed in the saddle making business. William Greenfield had two employees and William Sutherland worked with his son, also called William, and a journeyman. A third man, William Douglas, living at 18 High Street, also gave his occupation as a saddler but does not appear in the 1852 trade directory. There were three journeymen saddlers and one apprentice. As three of these are accounted for in the employment of the two established saddlers, it may be that William Douglas employed the other one.

Summary

Tanning appears to have been in decline at this time: the number of tanners was falling and the workforce was aging. In contrast, currying remained in much the same state as in 1841: employment numbers were level and young people were coming in as apprentices. Glue making was very much a growth industry and had overtaken tanning in terms of employment levels. In all three of these industries local people and families remained dominant.

Agriculture

As we have seen, the Industrial Revolution had already had an impact on Linlithgow by the middle of the nineteenth century. However, there were still many agricultural tasks which required to be done by hand. These varied in their skill level with a spectrum running from those which required expertise developed over many years to those which required raw muscle power, and lots of it. Of course, some improvements in agriculture were as a result of better techniques rather than the introduction of new machinery. Linlithgow came in for mention in an article in the Aberdeen Journal:

> 'A Correspondent, who has made a tour lately through various parts of the Lothians, and the counties of Linlithgow, Stirling and Clackmannan, and made extensive inquiries regarding the potatoe (sic) and turnip crops, writes us that, in almost every instance, the potatoes are keeping much better than in any of the past years since the failure of 1845... "In some parts," he says, "the farmers have adopted what occurs to me to be an improved system of storing from that practised through Aberdeen and the northern counties of Scotland." '[99]

The life of the countryside was intimately linked with that of the town. The countryside provided food supplies for the town. The town provided services and manufactured goods for the residents of the countryside. That said, a farm in the right location could look to the wider world. This is illustrated by a small ad in the Glasgow Herald from Friday 24th January 1851 for the lease of Pardovan Farm:

> 'It is situated in a very desirable locality, about three miles to the east of the county town. It is intersected by the Union Canal, as well as the Edinburgh and Glasgow Railway, and as there are both a Landing Wharf and Railway Depot close to the Farm Steading, the facilities for conveying produce to market, and bringing manure to the Farm are such as are seldom to be met with.' [100]

Offers were to be made 'wholly in money, or partly in money and partly in grain' to the owner or the current leaseholder, Mr Glen, Writer (solicitor) in Linlithgow.

From an employment point of view, there was no clear distinction between town and countryside when it came to working in agriculture. It was not uncommon for people who lived within the town to work in agriculture-related jobs and for people who lived outside the town boundaries to come into the town to work. Baillie had found, in the 1841 census, 44 agricultural labourers living in the town, showing that the there was no dividing line between the two when it came to occupations.[101] It must also be borne in mind that this was an age in which people were much less pigeonholed into one form of employment or another

---

99   The Aberdeen Journal, 24th December 1851
100   Glasgow Herald, 24th January 1851
101   Baillie, p19-20

than they are today. A child who lived on a farm may have been recorded as a scholar but would still have been expected to help out on the farm. At busy periods of year, especially at harvest time, many people would have been drawn into the Linlithgow countryside from the burgh as well as from outwith the parish: the census data does not enable us to measure this activity. What it does give us is a large number of people who explicitly state a form of employment related to agriculture and a group of people for whom the Occupation field was used to record their relationship to one of the farmers, farm servants, agricultural labourers etc., for example 'Son of Farmer' or 'Wife of Farm Servant'. Those men and women who were explicitly employed in agriculture related occupations are tabulated in Table 8. Those people aged thirteen or over who were implicitly employed are recorded in Table 9.

Across the parish the agricultural sector employed the most men, ahead even of shoemaking, and the second most women after those who were servants. Along with the retail and textiles sectors it was one of the three areas of the economy that employed large number of both sexes. So what were they doing or, at least, how were they described?

Table 8: Formally employed in agriculture

Male		Female	
Labourer	191	Labourer	75
Farm Servant	116	Cowfeeder/keeper	10
Farmer	48	Farm Servant	6
Ploughman	8	Farmer	5
Cowfeeder	5	Dairymaid	4
Shepherd	5		
Miller	5		
Grazier	2		
Steward	2		
Grieve	1		
Hedger	1		
Total	384		100

Table 9. People aged thirteen or over implicitly working in agriculture

Male		Female	
Son	12	Wife	35
		Daughter	13
		Sister	3
		Mother	1
		Mother-In-Law	1
Total	12		53

Adding the people in the two tables together gives us a total of 549 people working in agriculture. Though this will be closer to the true total than simply taking the figures in table 8 it still does not capture those who worked seasonally or other adult family members who contributed but whose occupations were left blank.

Returning to the more secure figures in Table 8, at the top of sector we find 48 male and five female farmers. Between them they employed over 400 people. It is clear that, the Agricultural Revolution notwithstanding, this was still a labour intensive industry with the majority of the workers being labourers. The proportion of male servants on farms may appear to be completely at odds with what we find for servants in the town. The title is, in fact, somewhat misleading, as a farm servant was someone who was under contract to a farmer to work for him or her for a specified period of time, rather than someone who was undertaking domestic work. Of course, most farms had domestic servants working in the farm house. They were recorded in the same style as a servant working in the house of any of the other better off families, making it clear that the role of farm servant was considered to be different.

The job titles in Table 8 suggest a greater degree of specialisation than was probably the case. Farm servants would undertake whatever work the farmer required on the farm and could thus be ploughmen, cowfeeders and so on as the situation demanded.

Not surprisingly there is a big difference in the make-up of the labour force compared to those involved in the shoe and leather industries. While they were dominated by locals, agriculture was dominated by incomers. Just 34% of the men and 35% of the women working in agriculture were born in the parish.

Agriculture would appear to be the type of sector in which it would be relatively easy for a person to seek employment in a distant area; every county in Scotland had farms, skills were transferable and there was a lot of work to be done. In practise this does not seem to have been the case; rather the country seems to have segmented into different markets for agricultural labour: Scottish incomers to Linlithgow parish working in agriculture came almost exclusively from the rest of West Lothian, Midlothian and Stirlingshire (mostly from Muiravonside). Not even nearby Lanarkshire provided more than five people. The exception to this rule was Ireland which provided 22% of male and 15% of female agricultural sector workers. Contracts, or fees, were usually for six months (running between the two 'term days' – Martinmas and Candlemas) after which time a farm servant could find employment elsewhere for the next half year if he or she wanted a change, or if the farmer didn't wish to retain them. This led to a workforce which was often on the move (as late as the 1950s my brother-in-law attended twelve different schools as his father's farm work moved the family round Angus). It seems likely that West Lothian formed part of a farming labour market along with the nearer parts of Midlothian and Stirlingshire. It would be interesting to see figures for the birthplaces of farm workers in these areas at this time. Perhaps even more surprising is the degree to which the farmers themselves were incomers. Farming is an occupation where one might expect a good deal of continuity at the upper levels yet only 24 (45%) of the farmers were born in the parish. Admittedly most of the incomers had not travelled far: 23 were from other parts of West Lothian, Midlothian or Stirlingshire (again predominantly Muiravonside with six out of eight). The picture of families farming the land for generations does not seem to hold true in this area at that time. It should be noted that the census data does not give information on property ownership. As such, it does not tell us how many of the farmers rented their farms. Those who rented may have been more likely to move on rather than stay in one place during their working lives.

Agriculture was still a very manual sector. There were high levels of turnover of farms. Most farmers were incomers and this was even more pronounced amongst other workers. However, few had travelled far to undertake this kind of work. The local labour market for agriculture seems to have comprised West Lothian, the west of Midlothian and the east of Stirlingshire. The other significant contribution came from the Irish.

The Railways

The Railways sit alongside agriculture as a great employer of muscle. A series of events in 1850 show that it was not just the construction but also the operation of the railways that could be hazardous for those involved. On the 5th July a porter was killed in an accident moving coaches onto a siding[102]. On the 24th August three Irishmen men were killed in the construction of a bridge over the new Bo'ness to Slammanan branch line.[103] There was another fatality on the 20th September when the guard on the 10:30 Glasgow to Edinburgh express fell from the train while applying the brake as the train approached Linlithgow station. Even in these early days railway staff had to cope with antisocial behaviour from some of the passengers. On the 27th March Sir John Lauder was found guilty of damaging railway property between Linlithgow, where he and his party had boarded, and Edinburgh, and of assaulting the guard, who had tried to detain him when he returned to the devastated carriage to retrieve his top hat.[104] Another member of the party, Sir William Henry Don, was found not guilty (though he was admonished) of a long list of misdemeanours in Linlithgow station, including stealing the station master's bell, destroying or damaging various pieces of railway property, as well as setting off the alarm bell, locking the door of the telegraph office and throwing away the key![105]

Baillie's figures for 1841 show 293 general labourers resident in the town.[106] This figure would have included those working on the construction of the railway along with those working in other industries. In 1851 we find 270 of the men in Linlithgow parish worked on the railways, of whom 256 gave their occupation as 'railway labourer'. Ireland was the place of birth for 203 of these men and 32 came from the Highlands: only one Linlithgow born man worked as a railway labourer. Clearly there was a high demand for manual work on the railways: the number of people employed in this capacity is equivalent to the number of people labouring in the agriculture sector. What is less clear is what they were doing. The Edinburgh to Glasgow line had opened in 1842. There had been continued development of stations and branch lines through the rest of the decade, such as North Bridge Station (now Waverley) in 1846, the Musselburgh branch line (also opened in 1846) and the Shieldhill branch (opened in 1847).

---

102   *Glasgow Herald, 12th July 1850*
103   *Caledonian Mercury, 5th September 1850*
104   *Caledonian Mercury, 1st April 1850*
105   *Caledonian Mercury, 15th April 1850*
106   *Baillie, p19-20*

EMPLOYMENT

There had been entire new lines opened in the area such as the Carstairs-Edinburgh-Glasgow line (the northern part of the Caledonian Railway) in 1848 and the Edinburgh & Bathgate Railway in 1849. The Slammanan and Bo'ness railway was opened on the 17th March 1851, just two weeks before the night of the census. It seems unlikely that the men working on these and similar projects would have been resident in Linlithgow: railway construction required a flexible, itinerant workforce, not commuters. It is very striking that in Bathgate parish we find a substantial Irish community of 407 and yet only 18 of them are railway labourers, though the construction work had completed much more recently in that area.[107] In Bo'ness parish, the home of the newest railway in the county, there were only 36 men recorded with railway related jobs. It is possible that Linlithgow's position on the line made it a good location from which to direct and undertake maintenance work, however this is purely speculative.

Not surprisingly, railway labouring was predominantly a younger man's occupation. Although there were a few men in their 50s and three 60 year olds, the bulk were in their 20s and 30s and the average age was 28.

There were fourteen other people, all men, employed on the railways. Four were platelayers and four were porters. The others were a railway agent, a wagon greaser, an engine fitter, a clerk, a railway police officer and William Young the stationmaster, aged 51 from Perth. He lived at Railway Station House. The bulk of these were incomers though two of the platelayers and the railway agent were locals.

Many of the railway labourers lived in lodging houses (often run by Irish women). With low wages and the need for mobility this was probably the best solution to their accommodation needs.

Despite the large numbers involved in the upkeep of the railways, the numbers involved in equivalent work on the canal were miniscule. There were three labourers, one boatman and one collector of canal dues. All five were incomers. The roads come out even worse: maintaining them was one solitary road labourer.

The night of the 30th March 1851 found very high numbers of railway labourers in Linlithgow. These were typically young and Irish, though the Highlands were well represented. There is no clear reason why they were in the town at this time

---

107   *The most common Irish male employment in Bathgate in 1851 was coal mining.*

or for how long they remained. However, the presence of a number of lodging houses in the town, providing many of them with accommodation, suggests that this was more than a short term state of affairs.

Quarrying and Mining

In 1843 Andrew Bell had recorded that limestone was being excavated at Silvermine, Hillhouse and Carrubbers and that two stone quarries were in operation at Kingscavil and East Binny. In 1851 there were still substantial numbers of men employed in the quarries. A total of 26 men said they worked at a quarry, but only five recorded themselves as limestone miners.

Andrew Bell had mentioned thin seams of coal in the south of the parish that were at that time unworked. By 1851 this had changed with nine men employed in coal production. Neither Andrew Bell in 1843, nor Reverend Dobie in 1793, make any mention of iron ore, yet in 1851 we find twenty men employed in its extraction. The complement of 63 quarry and mine workers is made up by one man who is recorded as a miner without any more detailed information as to what it was he was digging up.

In terms of age, quarriers and miners were similar to railway workers. The average age was slightly older at 29 and there were very few men over 50.

In line with other labour intensive occupations, only a minority (twenty) came from within the parish. Almost as many (sixteen) came from Ireland. Other notable contingents came from the rest of West Lothian (seven), Midlothian (six) and Lanarkshire (four). The parish of Straith (Strath) in Skye provided three quarrymen, including Donald and Roderick Robertson who may have been brothers. It also supplied two railway labourers and a general labourer.

While limestone mining appears to have all but disappeared, stone quarrying was still a significant employer. Coal and iron ore mining had come into operation over the course of a few years. The number of coal miners was still low compared to other parishes: Linlithgow was never to be a major coal producing area. Miners and quarrymen were typically young incomers to the parish.

General Labourers

A significant proportion of the male employment pool declared themselves to be general labourers. These men would turn their hands to whatever manual work was required at the time and thus acted as a flexible temporary workforce across a number of industries. The 1851 census shows us that there were 93 men in Linlithgow Parish employed this way, as well as one foreman. Just over 30% of labourers were 50 or older: for many men it may have been too late to learn a new trade. The king of them all was of course 106 year old John Campbell.

It may be significant that the census was taken in March rather than in the autumn. Had it been, many of the general labourers could well have been employed in harvesting and might have given their occupations as agricultural labourers.

As with those involved in agriculture, the majority of general labourers were incomers. Only 36% were natives to the parish. The pattern of migration is very similar to agriculture with the rest of West Lothian, Midlothian, Stirlingshire and Ireland providing almost all of the others.

The number of general labourers was substantial but they were an aging population. Perhaps younger labourers were finding jobs within specific industries. Most of the men in this group were incomers, but few had travelled far.

Servants

a.   Domestic Service

For a woman in Linlithgow parish in 1851, by far the most common type of employment was as a servant. This was already the case in 1841 where Baillie reports 123 female and sixteen male domestic servants in the town.[108] In the 1851 census we find 456 people who were servants, of which 436 were women (46% of the female working population) and twenty were men. It seems unlikely that there had been a shortage of servants in 1841, and certainly there was no such indication in the New Statistical Account of 1843. Though Baillie's figures are purely for the town, and this volume covers the whole parish, it should be

---

108   *Baillie p23*

borne in mind that those people who described themselves as farm servants have been separated out and included under Agriculture. That the number of servants had more than trebled in the intervening decade suggests that demand had increased dramatically. This in turn would seem to suggest that the people of Linlithgow felt more affluent than ten years earlier.

It would appear that many women became servants as their first, and possibly last, jobs, working until they were married and/or could afford to stop. This was perhaps most true of local girls, who with 146 representatives made up a third of the female servants. Many of them were in their teens and their average age was 25. The average age of the 290 women servants who were incomers was 28. The following table shows all areas in which ten or more incoming women servants had been born.

The Dawsons, standing behind their Kellie in-laws, in a photograph thought to have been taken in June 1868. The white bearded John Dawson stands beside his wife Euphemia. Beside her stand their son, Adam, and one of his sisters, either Frances or Jane. The young woman in front of Adam is his wife, Helen (nee Kellie), holding their son John Kellie Dawson. The lady in the background is unidentified but there is a suggestion that it could be a nanny or similar. Could it be Ursula Sword? She would have been 47 years old when this photo was taken. Copyright Russ Sims

Table 10: Place of birth of female servants born outwith Linlithgow (areas with 10 or more)

	Number
Other West Lothian	93
Stirling	47
Midlothian	42
Ireland	32
Lanarkshire	15
Perthshire	11

It seems clear that Linlithgow acted as a magnet for young women in the surrounding parishes and counties. Its relatively affluent community offered opportunities for them to make a start in life.

Some servants, of course, held more prestigious positions than others. Housekeepers, governesses and cooks probably felt themselves to be a cut above house maids or laundry maids.

A total of 34 women were housekeepers. Having worked their way up through the system, they were older than most other servants: their average age was 41. As was the trend in many occupations, the proportion of Linlithgow born people was higher in the more senior positions. While only a third of female servants were born in the parish just short of half (sixteen) of the housekeepers were. Interestingly, the three governesses in the parish all came from England. The three cooks had not travelled quite so far though all were incomers: they hailed from Elgin, Cluny (in Argyll) and Larbert. Ursula Sword, aged 30, from South Leith was the only nursery governess in the parish. She lived with the Dawson family, owners of St Magdalene's Distillery at Green Park. The Dawsons had four children: Adam (aged eight), John (seven), Jane Douglas (five) and Frances McKell (three). Giving a child a middle name was a fashion amongst middle and upper classes. On the night of the census Green Park was home to the six Dawsons, three visitors, Ursula and three other servants (all female).

The male servants cover a diverse group of occupations: servant boy, servant, house servant, gentleman's servant, groom (two), and butler (two). One of the butlers, William Lardner, was born in Middlesex and now worked at Binny House. Henry Anderson, born in Bathgate, was butler at Preston House.

A small group of men worked in senior positions with outdoor responsibilities on the large estates. There were two gamekeepers, one overseer and two land stewards.

Nine of the male servants were from Linlithgow and thirteen were incomers. Three each came from Perth and East Lothian – both counties with many country houses.

b.   Gardening

Gardeners are hard to categorise as they may have been servants, attached to a big house, or they may have worked as part of a small business or on their own as independent tradesmen. Nineteen men from a variety of birth places are recorded as gardeners. One clue as to their activities may be that the 1856 Ordnance Survey map shows two nurseries to the east and west of Preston Road, just to the south of the railway line. The gardeners seem to be an aging group: after an eleven year old apprentice, the second youngest was 28 and the average age was 46. It would be interesting to know who the eleven year old, William McFarlane, was apprenticed to. Unfortunately all the census tells us is that his father was a baker and that he lived at home, in the West Port, with his seven brothers and sisters.

Five of the nineteen gardeners were local men, the same as the number from Midlothian. Alexander Robertson from Fetteresso in Kincardineshire described himself as a gentleman's gardener. He lived with his wife Helen in Teind Barn, which was near Strawberrybank – an area where there were no doubt some of the finest gardens in the town. The birth places of their three children suggest an itinerant lifestyle. Helen junior, aged four, was born in Banchory. Two years later Mary had been born in Cumbernauld and Louisa, who was yet to reach her first birthday, was born in Linlithgow. They had no servants.

c.   Mangle and Washer Women

Not everyone could afford to have servants but before the advent of the washing machine or launderette, there was the washerwoman and the laundress. With no machinery more sophisticated than a mangle, washing clothes and linen was a very time-consuming and labour intensive business. No doubt the idea of using the services of one of these women would be very attractive to those who could afford it.

In Linlithgow in 1851 there were fourteen women who worked in this field. Nine gave their occupation as washer or washerwoman (one was also a 'washer and sewer' who perhaps mended clothes as well as washing them), three gave their occupation as laundress, one was a manglewoman and one was a mangle keeper. Without wishing to read too much into what may be little more than a different choice of words, it may be that the washers, laundresses and housewives of the town paid the mangle keeper to allow them the use of her mangle while the manglewoman would have been paid to do the mangling for them.

The women in this sector were predominantly local. Nine were born in the parish while two more came from Bo'ness and one from Muiravonside. Their average age was just under 49 – quite old for such strenuous work.

Summary

Servants played a major role in the life of parish. The dramatic increase in the number of domestic servants suggests that Linlithgow was enjoying higher levels of prosperity than in 1841 and was attracting young women from neighbouring areas to meet demand. Local women were outnumbered roughly two to one in the servant community, but made up almost half of all housekeepers. The much smaller number of male servants appear to have worked principally at the large houses within the parish.

The age profile of the gardeners suggests a trade in decline while their places of birth suggest one which was not attractive to local men, or for which they lacked the skills.
Though not servants, strictly speaking, washerwomen no doubt played a significant role in easing the domestic burden. They tended to be local, older women.

Textile Related Employment

We have seen that textiles had enjoyed a long tradition within Linlithgow. In the Statistical Account of 1793, James Dobie wrote about the Printfield, recording that it had been founded in 1786, that employment had peaked at 200 and that though this was down by half 'at the time of the writing' there were hopes of revival. He also recorded two tambouring factories employing 86 girls. In 1841

Baillie found 23 calico printers[109] living within the burgh and in 1843 Andrew Bell reported that calico-printing was thriving but that the tambourers (cloth embroiderers) had fallen on hard times.

a.   Calico Printing

In 1851 we find that calico printing (decorative printing on cloth) continued to be a major employer in the parish, though nationally Linlithgow was no more than a bit part player in this field: the Leeds Mercury reported that, at this time, there were 31 cotton factories in Lanarkshire employing 7,388 people and a further 29 cotton factories in Renfrewshire.[110]

A bewildering array of occupations were given within the industry such as tearer, streamer, print cutter, block printer, colour maker, whitener, dyer, piece hanger, grounder, orange dyer, cans worker, and many who were just styled 'Printfield Worker'. Of these, the printers were considered to be skilled artisans, and paid accordingly.[111] The supporting roles were generally undertaken by low skilled, low paid workers.

It appears that many young people, especially women, started their working lives in textile manufacture. The 1851 census shows 61 women and 32 men under twenty working in manual jobs at what is described as the 'calico printfield', 'printworks', 'printfield' or just plain 'field'. In particular, textile manufacture seems to have been a source of employment for youngsters who had left school early, or perhaps had never attended school at all. In total, 22 of the employees were under thirteen years old.

All in all, the census shows that there were 90 women and 64 men employed in the calico business. Of these, 24 were printers – they were mostly men and two thirds came from Linlithgow. The remaining 130 undertook the lower skilled roles. Just in the minority were Linlithgow born people, with the second largest contingent coming from Ireland, as with most low skilled industries. At their head stood John Anderson, Cotton Manufacturer, 48 years old, born in Stirling and resident with his wife, son and two servants in Clarendon House. It may be that they had only recently arrived in Linlithgow since young David was less than a year old and was born in Wardie, Edinburgh.

---

109   *Baillie, p21*
110   *Leeds Mercury, Saturday 18th January 1851*
111   *Smout, ACOTSP, p21*

b.   Tambouring

Life continued to be tough for the tambourers. A group of 48 women remained in the town who gave their occupation as tambourers or muslin tambourers. With few new recruits their average age was going up and had now reached 45. Nearly 90% were born in the town – people did not move to Linlithgow to be tambourers. Where younger people were involved in the industry there was often a family connection. For example at 276 High Street we find a mother and daughter, both called Helen Somerville and both tambourers. Aged seventeen, the daughter was the youngest tambourer in the parish.

Andrew Bell had spoken of the penury of the tambourers and it is clear that they continued to live life close to the poverty line. In addition to the 48 people who gave their occupation as tambourers a further fifteen were described as 'pauper – tambourer'. Amongst paupers who gave an occupation this formed the largest group. The pauper tambourers were even older with an average age of just under 60.

c.   Weaving

Another occupation in terminal decline was handloom weaving. The steady march of the power loom through the first half of the nineteenth century eroded the livelihood of the weavers. To make matters worse, during the 1830s and `40s manufacturers found a new labour supply in the Irish who were willing, through necessity, to work for very low wages. T. C. Smout wrote 'The weavers began the 1780s as one of the most confident and affluent of all groups, and ended up in the 1830s appallingly depressed and pauperised. Theirs is the prime example of the decline and fall of a prosperous occupation in the years of industrialisation.'[112] This was a male occupation and one of the traditional, incorporated trades of the town, yet by 1851 it had almost been extinguished.

Baillie noted that in 1841 the town had an aging group of eighteen weavers.[113] Their decline had continued over the next ten years with the number reducing to eight. Those who remained in the trade were all male and aged between 41 and 70. In addition there were three people who were described in the census as 'pauper weaver', for whom the unequal battle to make a living seems to have become too much.

---

112   *Smout, AHOTSP, p393*
113   *Baillie, p22*

d.   Dressmaking

If the preparation of material was in decline, the same is not true of those jobs which took material and turned it into finished goods. Most dramatic is the rise in the number of women employed in dressmaking. From eighteen in 1841 this rose to 49 in 1851. Dressmakers had thus overtaken tambourers. Unlike them they were more prosperous (there is only one pauper dressmaker) and much younger with an average age of 28. In another contrast with the tambourers, almost half (22) had moved into the parish. The most common places of origin were Ireland, Midlothian and other parts of West Lothian.

e.   Hat and Bonnet Making

Along with an increase in the supply (and presumably the demand) for new dresses came an increase in the production of new hats. Back in 1841 there was one milliner and two straw hat makers. In 1851 three young ladies were milliners, Lillias Porteous (nineteen) and Elizabeth Calder (24) in the High Street and Ann Hardie (25) at the Low Port, while four more were either makers of straw hats or straw bonnets, which were presumably the same thing.

f.   Tailors

Comparative data for tailoring businesses

Pigot's Trade Directory (1837)	10
Slater's Trade Directory (1852)	12

Going slightly against this trend were the tailors. Their number had declined slightly from 28 in 1841 to 23 in 1851. This runs contrary to the evidence from the trade directories. It may be that the average size of a tailor's business had become slightly smaller. In terms of age, the tailors seem to be well distributed. There were four youths aged thirteen to seventeen in the trade and the average age was 36.

The most unusual feature of the tailors, when compared to the long established incorporated trades and the equivalent female occupations, is that there were slightly more incomers than natives: twelve to eleven. Ireland, Midlothian and Stirling each provided three tailors.

g.   Seamstresses

Seamstresses made, altered and mended clothes. They may have worked in part with the dressmakers or tailors. In 1851 we find nineteen of them in Linlithgow. Although there are no seamstress paupers, the age profile suggests that this was an occupation in decline. Of the twelve Linlithgow born seamstresses, the youngest was 26, though there were two younger women from Ireland. The average of 42.5 is much higher than the dressmakers or tailors and not far short of the tambourers.

h.   Clothes Brokers

Finally, when it came to the supply of clothing, the town had two clothes brokers: Catherine Devlin and William Moreland, both from Ireland. The only two other clothes brokers in West Lothian at the time were an Irish husband and wife living in Bo'ness. Were they traders of second hand clothes?

i.   Drapers

The drapers were dealers in cloth and cloth goods. Although Baillie makes no mention of drapers in 1841 they formed a small but not insignificant part of the Linlithgow workforce in 1851. Unusually, drapers could be male or female. The eleven people whose employment was in this field comprised six drapers (four men and two women), three apprentices, one assistant and a draper's salesman. Most were incomers: the only three locals were two young apprentices and the assistant. Other than the two female drapers the rest of the group were men. John Kirsopp, aged 44 and born in England, was also a magistrate, showing that drapers could be substantial figures within the town.

The drapers and clothes brokers are sufficiently removed from the production of textiles that they could equally well be considered to sit under 'Commerce'.

Summary

Calico printing was thriving and provided low skilled work for the young (in particular if they were locals or of Irish origin). Tambouring and handloom weaving were nearing their end and employed fewer and older people than ten years previously. Dressmaking and millinery were on the up and tailoring seems to have been in a slight decline. Drapers seem to have been growing with a good proportion of apprentices learning skills from experienced incomers.

Construction and Manufacturing

a.   The Building Trades

In the 1841 census Baillie found 90 residents of the town who gave their employment as masons.[114] The demand for masons at that time was no doubt related to the construction of the railway. By 1851 we find that the number had declined to 60 and there were few people learning the trade.

Two men styled themselves as master masons: William Malcolm (32) from Muiravonside and James Mackie (56) from Uphall. A group of 23 men were simply masons and the same number were journeymen. There were only two men (aged fifteen and sixteen) who were apprentices. The remaining ten were mason's labourers.

Just 38% of masons were born in the parish, a not dissimilar percentage to agriculture and general labourers. The rest came from a variety of parts of the country with the only areas to provide more than two men being Ireland (fourteen) and the rest of West Lothian (nine).

Working alongside the masons were a number of other trades. The 1841 census contains nine slaters, seven house painters and three plasterers in the burgh.[115] In 1851 the numbers for the parish were seven, four and one respectively, although the census data indicates that a proportion of the people were multi-skilled. Additionally there was one builder and one plumber. Like the masons, this suggests a general decline in these trades from 1841. Unlike the masons, these trades were dominated by local men. Only three had been born outside the parish: two from Bo'ness and one from Dalmeny.

The building trades had declined since the completion of the railway. Masons were generally incomers but those undertaking other trades in this sector were mostly natives.

b.   Wood and Metal Working

In mid-Victorian Britain the two principal materials from which artefacts or implements were made were wood and metal. These were of course produced

---

114   *Baillie, p17*
115   *Baillie, p17*

using traditional local skills. Due to the long standing importance of the smiths and the wrights they were two of the incorporated trades with a place on the town council. With over 100 men in these two fields of employment in 1851 it is clear that there was still considerable demand for on the spot production and repair of wooden and metal items.

While it almost certain that these men carried out most of their work in the vicinity of Linlithgow, some of them may well have plied their trade further afield on occasions. There is certainly evidence of wood and metal workers being brought into the town. In 1850 Adam and John Dawson, the distillers, took Messers John Angus and Brothers, millwrights and engineers from Rosyth, to court over failure to complete a contract for alterations and repairs to the Bonnytoun Grinding Mills.[116]

The different branches of woodworking employed 67 men. The traditional Scottish word for a woodworker was a wright. In the 1841 census Baillie found men termed as 'joiner' or 'wright' and by 1851 we find that 'carpenter' has joined the lexicon. Though all were doing the same sort of work, it may be significant that it was, on average, the younger men who called themselves carpenters (the most recently introduced term) while the oldest average age of the three were those who called themselves wrights.

Slater's Trade Directory followed Pigot in listing 'Wrights' and the census data shows that these older men, at the top of the trade, did indeed call themselves wrights. However, the usage was not simply down to age or seniority as some young men called themselves apprentice wrights.

Comparative Data for Wrights Businesses

Pigot's Trade Directory (1837)	4
Slater's Trade Directory (1852)	7

A poem of 1855 gives a description of the work of a man called John Wright the Joiner:

> *'With industry he plied his useful art;*
> *He'd make a spinning-wheel or mend a cart;*
> *Make tables, chairs, or anything of wood,*

---

116   *Caledonian Mercury, 25th July 1850*

No matter what; the workmanship was good.[117]

There seems to have been a 'changing of the guard' since 1837. In 1841 Baillie had found that the men who called themselves wrights had an average age of 50.[118] By 1851 a new generation was in place, including a number of apprentices. Comparing the entries in Pigot against those in Slater, we find that of the four wrights listed by the former in 1837 only one name, that of John Landels appears in the list of seven wrights in business in Linlithgow in 1852. Even this may not have been the same man. There were two John Landels living in Linlithgow in the 1851 census. Both were born in different parts of Berwickshire and may well have been father and son. The older, aged 56, styled himself in the 1851 census as 'bailie and builder employing twenty six'. He could be the wright from 1837 and possibly the 1852 directory. However, there is also an entry in Slater's for John Landels, builder. Would he be in twice? This second entry seems a better match. The younger John Landels was 28 in 1851 and gave himself in the census as a house carpenter. Had he redefined himself to wright the following year? He certainly could not have been the 1837 version. What is clear is that Landels senior, a wright or former wright, was an important man in the town. As well as being one of the bailies on the council, he was the burgh's commissioner to the General Assembly of the Church of Scotland.

The number of men termed wrights, joiners or carpenters came to 59 in total. Of these, five seem to have been specialists: we find one cartwright, one sievewright, one housewright and three millwrights.

Of the other 53, nine were apprentices, of whom seven came from Linlithgow, one from Torphichen and the ninth from Brora in Sutherland. They were aged between fourteen and eighteen. The youngest was David Dunn, the boy from Brora. Young David was living with his uncle, also David Dunn. David senior, himself a joiner, had not been born in Sutherland but in Anstruther in Fife, suggesting a very mobile family. From the ages and birth places of his children he appears to have lived in Linlithgow for at least 24 years.

There were 21 journeymen of whom twelve came from Linlithgow and the rest from locations scattered across the country. Their average age was 34.

The remaining 23 men went under a variety of descriptions such as 'joiner', 'carpenter', 'joiner wright', 'house carpenter', 'wright' or 'house wright'. They were

117   Lothian, p7
118   Baillie, p15

split eleven to twelve between locals and incomers. Their average age was 40. Though one man was styled a 'master joiner' and one a 'master wright' the term 'master' does not seem to have been as widely used as in other trades.

Between them, the joiners, carpenters and wrights comprised 59 of the 67 men in the category of wood workers. To complete the list we need to record the other eight men. Six were down at the bottom end of the pile; sawyers, or 'sawyers of wood'. Thomas Veitch from Musselburgh was a 'lath splitter and riddlemaker'. Lathsplitters were involved in the building trade: laths being narrow strips of wood used to provide a framework to support plasterwork. A riddle, of course, is a sort of coarse sieve used with grain, soil or similar items. Very much at the refined end of woodworking was Charles Douglas, a cabinet maker from Cramond. His competition from 1841, William Kirk, was no longer in West Lothian, or at least not on the night of the census.

Comparative Data for Blacksmiths

Pigot's Trade Directory (1837)	1
Slater's Trade Directory (1852)	7

In 1851 we find 34 men within the parish working metal. Of these, 29 describe themselves as blacksmith or smith, compared with seventeen in the burgh found by Baillie from the 1841 census.[119] Additionally, one man was a coppersmith, one was a tinsmith, one was both a copper and a tinsmith and two were nailers. The last of these represents a big decrease from the seven nailers found by Baillie in the 1841 census.[120] Given that the amount of woodworking appears to have been very much on the increase, who was making the nails? Perhaps they were being manufactured elsewhere and brought into the town.

Four young Linlithgow men aged between fourteen and eighteen were apprentice blacksmiths and at the other end four men described themselves as master blacksmiths.

Just over half (nineteen) of the metal workers came from Linlithgow. The rest came from a variety of areas with four originating in other parts of West Lothian, three from Midlothian and two from Stirlingshire. The average age of men in the metalworking trades was 39 but this hides a significant difference between locals

---

119   Baillie, p14
120   Baillie, p14

(average age 34) and incomers (average age 45). This may indicate a tradition of incomers completing their apprenticeship at their place of birth before moving to Linlithgow, and hence being older, on average, than the locals.

The number of men engaged in wood and metal working appears to have increased substantially since 1841. Just over half of the men came from Linlithgow. The others may have been attracted by increased demand for their skills and the increased opportunity to trade within the burgh. Young men, predominantly local, seem to have seen wood working as a trade worth entering.

c.   **Engineering**

Five men come under this category. Three describe themselves as engineers and one as a civil engineer. The fifth is an engine keeper, which may mean that he acted as a mechanic. It is unclear how one progressed one's career to become an engineer. The civil engineer, whose work may have been related to railway construction, was aged 42 and the rest were between 26 and 36. Only one was locally born. Looking at other people in West Lothian described as engineers in the census, the largest number, seven, are found in Bo'ness, where the railway to Slamannan had just opened.

d.   **Papermaking**

Papermaking was a growing industry. John Butt wrote 'In the first half of the nineteenth century paper-making expanded considerably. In 1868 Scotland possessed fifty-seven paper mills of which twenty-two were in Midlothian.'[121]

In 1843 Andrew Bell had noted a paper mill on the River Avon in full employment, producing a considerable quantity of paper by machinery. This was the Lochmill, which had been converted to papermaking in 1808 by Thomas Kilgour. His gravestone, at St. Michael's Church, tells us that Thomas Kilgour, paper manufacturer, Lochmill, died in 1840 aged 70. The machinery mentioned by Andrew Bell was introduced in 1838 by the then owner, James Williamson, bring to an end 30 years of making paper by hand. It may have been because of changes in the method of production that many of the workforce in 1851, especially the most skilled men, were incomers. At the top of the industry stood James Williamson's successor, Robert Drennan of Bonhard Lodge, paper manufacturer. He was 32 years old and born in Tarbolton. There is no sign of

---

121   *Butt, p21*

Andrew Scott, Drennan's partner at the mill, in the census. It is possible that either he was away from home on the night of the 30th March, or that he lived outside the parish.

It is clear that this was a significant industry at this time, with the census recording 52 people (plus Drennan) employed in it in the town and environs. It seems to have had a number of similarities with the calico print works: both employed a mix of men and women, both had a base of unskilled young people and both had a substantial proportion of Irish workers. It seems likely that a number of people from Muiravonside would have come into the parish to work and the paper mill and the calico printfield would have been two of the most accessible employers.

Under Scott and Drennan worked 35 women and seventeen men. The women gave a number of occupations. Many were simply factory labourers or paper mill workers, others were rag cutters. Almost half of the women (seventeen) came from the parish. Their average age was 21 and most were in their teens. There were nine from Ireland, with the same average age. The other nine came from a variety of places. One was from the Highlands and the birth place of two was unknown (Highlands and 'Unknown' were often good sources of low skilled labour!) These nine were a little older with an average age of 28.

The less prestigious male jobs included clerk, bleacher, worker and labourer. Of the nine males in this group most were teenagers, or younger (there were two boys aged ten and eleven). The bleacher was 30 and then at the other end of the age spectrum there were two much older men, aged 55 and 70, who gave themselves as a factory labourer and a paper mill worker.

More skilled appear to have been those who were 'paper makers'. There were eight of these with an average age of 31. Bearing in mind Butt's comments at the start of this section it is understandable that half of the paper makers had come from Midlothian. Since the eighteenth century the Esk valley in particular had been a major centre for paper making[122] so it is no surprise that three of the men in this role came from Lasswade and Penicuik.

Only five of the seventeen men were from the parish, and these were mostly young lads: only one local man was a papermaker. Despite the presence of a number of Irish women there was only one Irish man and none from the Highlands.

---

122   *Shaw, p369*

Papermaking had arrived in the town early in the nineteenth century and was endeavouring to keep pace with technological changes in the industry. It was a significant employer in 1851 with a skills and employment profile similar to calico printing.

e.　Ropemaking

In 1837 Pigot's Trade Directory contained an entry for Robert McCall, rope maker. In 1852 Slater recorded that he was still in operation. In the 1851 Census we find McCall and two other men (possibly his employees) engaged in rope making, as well as one rope spinner and one in the related craft of mat making. McCall came from Falkirk and the other three rope men were from Midlothian. The birth place of the mat maker was unknown.

f.　Basketmaking

The only basket maker in the town was John Kirk from Ireland. This was not a trade deemed worthy of inclusion in the trade directories.

g.　Soap

William McGregor of 4 The Cross was a soap boiler. He seems to have been reasonably successful since his wife did not work, their three children aged seven to thirteen were all scholars and the older two daughters were also not employed. Soap was also produced as a by-product of glue making, for which see above.

h.　Candlemaking

In 1837 Pigot's Trade Directory contained an entry for Malcolm Adam, candlemaker. Now aged 84, Adam continued to ply his trade and to be the only candlemaker in the parish. He wasn't the only or the oldest one in the county, however: there were six others of whom 88 year old James Brown in Bathgate was the longest of tooth.

Brewing and Distilling

Comparative Data for Coopers and Maltsters Businesses

	Coopers	Maltsters
Pigot's Trade Directory (1837)	3	0
Slater's Trade Directory (1852)	2	2

We have seen that Linlithgow had a long history of commercial brewing and distilling with Reverend Dobie reporting three breweries and four distilleries in 1793, and Andrew Bell talking, in 1843, of a brewery and a 'very extensive distillery'. In 1851 both brewing and distilling continued though employment levels were not high.

The St Magdalene's whisky distillery was owned by John Dawson, aged 52, born in Linlithgow and living at Green Park with his family and servants (including Ursula Sword, the nursery governess whom we met under domestic servants). His father, Provost Adam Dawson, had been responsible for relocating the distillery in 1834 and had died in 1836 aged 88.[123] Green Park was on the Edinburgh Road, almost opposite the distillery. The site was later to become a petrol station, which has now been demolished in its turn.

John's entry in the census says that he employed 29 men. It is difficult to establish who they all were. Nine men say they were working as labourers at the distillery, one was a journeyman distiller and one man worked there as a clerk, making a total of eleven. The eight maltmen, or maltsters, could also have been employed at either establishment. However, two of them are listed in the 1852 trade directory and were thus, at least to some extent, independent businessmen. Some of the five coopers in the town (down from seven in 1841[124]) no doubt supplied the distillery, but could have been employed at the brewery, or elsewhere. Two of them are also listed in Slater's. Even if all of the above were included in John Dawson's figure, that only brings the total to 24. Several possible solutions to the gap between the figures occur. Firstly, it may well be that the remaining unaccounted for people were either labourers or carters: the transportation of the raw materials and finished product must have required considerable effort, and carters could well have categorised themselves as such

---

123   Mitchell & Mitchell, p32
124   Baillie, p18

without reference to what they were carrying. Secondly, it is possible that some of John Dawson's employees lived and/or worked outside the parish, perhaps in Edinburgh or Glasgow, or were absent on the night of the census.

Examining the people who we know worked either at the distillery or in related trades, half came from Linlithgow and half were incomers. The incomers dominated the unskilled elements with seven of the nine labourers. The locals dominated the skilled trades with six of the eight maltmen and three of the five coopers. The coopers, it should be remembered, were one of the incorporated trades with a place on the town council. While the distillery had need of them they survived, but their days were numbered. Edinburgh and Glasgow were both major centres of barrel production which would increasingly crowd out coopers in other central belt towns. While the railway created opportunities for the distillery and the brewery, it was not necessarily a benefit to all their employees.

As for brewing, the census only clearly identifies five individuals; a brewer, a clerk, two carters and an ale bottler. As noted above, some job titles were common between brewing and distilling making it unclear where an individual worked. All of them, high or low status, were incomers. Assuming that the brewery was the same one shown on the 1856 OS map, it was located at the west end of the High Street, at what is now the entrance to St John's Avenue.

Of the alcohol producing industries, distilling remained strong, using for the most part locals in the skilled roles and incomers to provide muscle power. The distillery remained in the hands of the Dawsons, a powerful family for several generations. Brewing skills were provided by incomers.

Commerce

Linlithgow was, and always had been, a market town. It was the commercial centre of West Lothian. Even with the coming of the train and reduced travel times it is hard to believe that many, if any, people went into Edinburgh or Glasgow for their shopping. As such, it is no surprise to find that many people in Linlithgow had retail related jobs.

The passing of the 1846 Burgh Trading Act had opened up the town to entrepreneurs from outside the town and a number had taken advantage of this to establish businesses. One major difference from the High Street today is that there were no chain stores. All the shops were owned locally.

The shops of the town provided the population of the town and surrounding area with the necessities and the luxuries of life. One of the basic necessities is of course food, which could be purchased at one of the many bakers, fleshers (butchers) or grocers shops. Alcohol, while not a necessity, was very much a part of life within the town, as can be seen by the number of spirits dealers. A number of other groups will be dealt with at the end of the section.

a.   Baking

Comparative Data for Bakers

Pigot's Trade Directory (1837)	10
Slater's Trade Directory (1852)	12

Linlithgow had a long tradition in baking. The bakers were one of the nine incorporated trades in the mediaeval council and we saw in the 1793 Statistical Account that the town's bakers exported as far as Queensferry. In the 1841 census Baillie found seventeen bakers[125] while in 1851 we find a total of 44 people working in bakery businesses.

At the top of the trade were three master bakers (one of whom was also a spirit dealer) and twelve bakers. Locals, or near locals, dominated with nine of these fifteen coming from the parish, as well as one from Torphichen and two from Bo'ness. The average age of the bakers and master bakers was 40. One surname that was to become well known and survive to the present day was that of Oliphant. John, aged 29, had moved from Torphichen and set up in business (the Oliphant's that still trades in the High Street today would not be set up until 1856). Deserving of recognition is Isabella Duncan – the town's only female baker in a male dominated profession. She lived at 245 High Street with her two daughters Elizabeth (27) and Alison (25), a servant, two apprentice bakers and a journeyman.

The nineteen journeymen bakers were also predominantly local. Only three came from outside the county. Thirteen were from Linlithgow and the other three were from Bo'ness.

---

125   *Baillie, p13*

The ten apprentices were aged between ten and nineteen. Once again they were mostly local: seven came from Linlithgow, one from Bo'ness, one from Kirkliston and the tenth only from as far as Edinburgh.

Overall it is clear that baking was very much in the control of local families with approximately two thirds coming from the parish.

b.   Fleshing

Comparative Data for Fleshing Businesses

Pigot's Trade Directory (1837)	6
Slater's Trade Directory (1852)	6

Like the bakers, the fleshers were another of the nine incorporated trades. In the 1841 census Bailey found twelve people in the burgh working as fleshers. In 1851 we find eleven in the parish: seven men who describe themselves specifically as fleshers, two journeyman fleshers and one who called himself a butcher. The eleventh was Alexander Forgie, from Muiravonside, who described himself as a 'flesher and grocer', while another Muiravonsider, Jane Roberts, may well have worked for him as she is described as a 'flesher's shopkeeper'. Finally there were two young lads each described as a 'flesher's boy' and a third one described as a 'butcher's boy'. In total that meant fifteen people involved in the trade, of whom eleven could be described as fleshers. This may indicate a slight decline in the fortunes of the fleshers, although we see in Slater that there was the same number of businesses as fifteen years earlier.

Fleshing seems to have been in the hands of relatively local families. Of the fifteen people, six come from Linlithgow, six from Muiravonside, two from Bo'ness and one from Carriden.

c.   Food and Drink

Comparative Data for Grocers & Spirit Dealers

	Grocers & Spirit Dealers	Vintners & Spirit Dealers
Pigot's Trade Directory (1837)	19	29
Slater's Trade Directory (1852)	26	32

T. C. Smout wrote:

> 'Drink was important in nineteenth-century Scotland. It was consumed in enormous quantities. In the 1830s, the population aged fifteen and over was drinking, on average, the equivalent of a little under a pint each of duty-charged whisky a week. There was no legal restriction on who might buy drink, and drunkenness among quite young apprentices and women was taken for granted. There was even a recognized problem of children drinking spirits under the age of fifteen.' [126]

Throughout this book we have been attempting to identify how many men and women worked at different times in the different occupations which made up the economy. The area in which this proved most difficult to unravel and break down is that of the supply of food and drink, and more specifically the supply of alcohol. As we shall see, there was no shortage of places in which to buy alcohol in Linlithgow at this time. The difficulty comes from the multiple roles taken on by people in this sector. As the Gazette journalist observed in the 1901 series of retrospective articles: '...in 1851 the trade of publican was mostly carried on as an adjunct of some other employment.'[127] A wide variety of job descriptions were in use, in a wider variety of combinations, making it difficult to categorise people effectively. Some people described their occupation in the census as publican, innkeeper, hotel keeper or tavern keeper, which seems fairly straight forward. Many used the term 'spirit dealer', often in combination with another form of employment. To add to the confusion, in the two trade directories the spirit dealers were grouped either with grocers or vintners. The figures from Slater are hard to reconcile with the data from the 1851 census (see Table 11 below).

---

126   Smout, ACOTSP, p133
127   Linlithgowshire Gazette, 19th April 1901, p4

Table 11. People specifying employment related to grocers & spirit dealers, Linlithgow 1851

Traders	Female	Male	Total
Grocer & Spirit Dealer/Merchant	2	1	3
Grocer	8	7	15
Small Grocer	5	0	5
Spirit Dealers/Merchant	3	7	10
Grocer & …	1	4	5
Victual or Provision Dealer/Merchant	2	3	5
Total	**22**	**28**	**50**
Shop Workers			
Grocer's Shopkeeper	2	0	2
Assistant Grocer	1	0	1
Assistant Grocer & Spirit Dealer	1	0	1
Total	**4**	**0**	**4**

Even adding all the traders in the top section of Table 11 together the total only comes to 50 yet Slater recorded 55 individuals under the two headings (he listed 58 but three of the names appeared in both sections). The gap can be bridged by including the seven publicans, inn, tavern and hotel keepers. Whatever the reason for the differences in the numbers may be, one thing is clear – there were an astonishing number of places in Linlithgow in which one could purchase food and/or drink. If the butchers and bakers (of whom four were licensed) are included, there were over 70 food and drink outlets in the town, or one for every 84 people in the entire parish! One final piece of evidence comes from the Gazette article quoted above which informs us that in 1851 there were 43 people in the burgh (of whom six were women) who held alcohol licenses, a number which swelled to 48 the following year. Though this does not enable us to calculate totals for the number of people employed in the different parts of the food and drink sector, it shows that alcohol formed a large part of it in a variety of guises.

One final sentence from the Gazette article makes interesting reading:

> *'The common practice of granting licences to smithies, which was made illegal by the Forbes Mackenzie Act of 1853, does not seem to have prevailed in Linlithgow.'*

One wonders why it was thought that alcohol, fire, red hot metal and heavy machinery made an obvious combination?

Going back to Table 11, it shows that five people gave themselves as being a grocer and something else. The combinations all seem to make sense:

Alexander Hardie	27	Master Currier and Grocer
David Nicol	37	Corn Merchant/Grocer
Alexander Morrison	38	Grocer and Currier
Agnes Sutherland	52	Grocer and Publican
Walter Glen	64	Merchant and Grocer

Agnes Sutherland is one of the group of women who had carved out a successful career within the town. In Slater she came within the Grocers & Spirit Dealers. She lived with her grown up son, who has no employment recorded against him but may have worked for her, and her daughter, a dressmaker. The ages of her children suggest that she had moved to Linlithgow from Kirknewton aged at most 21. The family lived, and may have worked, at 274 High Street – part of the street which was redeveloped in the 1960s.

Cross and Crosswell looking south c. 1870

Returning to the grocers and spirit dealers, it is notable that men and women were involved in almost equal numbers, though some of the categories were dominated by one or other of the sexes. An indication of the standing of the shopkeepers is that grocer John Hutton was also the town treasurer.

The people covered in Table 11 largely came from Linlithgow with locals outnumbering incomers by 28 to fifteen. This fits the pattern of traditional and higher status areas of employment remaining in the hands of the established inhabitants.

In terms of age, the people in this group are very well spread. Unlike more labour intensive occupations it was possible to be a shopkeeper well into old age. The average age was 44 with several people in their 70s and the oldest of all was Robert Easton, 80, of 20 West Port.

Table 12. People specifying employment related to public houses and hotels, Linlithgow 1851

Occupation	Female	Male	Total
Manager/Owner			
Publican/Innkeeper/Hotel Keeper/Tavern Keeper	1	6	7
Staff			
Hostler	0	2	2
Barmaid	1	0	1
Assistant in inn	1	0	1
Waiter	0	2	2
Cook (in hotel)	1	0	1
Total	**4**	**10**	**14**

Table 12 shows that a further fourteen people were involved in supplying drink and, to a lesser extent, food to the populace. Only three of them came from Linlithgow, though a further three came from other parts of West Lothian and two more from Muiravonside. No two of the rest had come from the same county.

The town's principal hotel, the Star and Garter, was in the hands of William Lawson, 29, from Dunbar. He had only recently taken over the reins. It is interesting to see how the newspapers were harnessed to effect the change of management and act as advertising for the new owner. The hotel was advertised in the Glasgow Herald on Monday 20th January 1851:

'To Let, Entry Immediately
In consequence of the death of the late Mr James Burleigh.

The Star and Garter Hotel, Linlithgow, which is an excellent House, (well frequented), and comfortably furnished with Stabling, Coach Horses, &c.

The incoming Tenant may get the whole of the Furnishing, Silver Plate, Bed and Table Linen, Wines and Spirits; also the Horses and Carriages at a   Valuation.

Apply to Mr. Glen, Writer, Linlithgow; or John Taylor & Son, Upholsterers, Assembly Rooms, Edinburgh.' [128]

On the 1st March William Lawson announced in the Scotsman that he had taken over the lease, and had 'selected his WINES, BRANDIES, &c., from one of the first-class houses in Edinburgh, so that the public may rely on every article being of the first-class description.'[129]

He seems to have chosen well, or had a good relation with the press. The Scotsman carried a notice on the 20th March, ten days before the census was taken, recording his opening dinner, attended by 'upwards of 60 men connected with the neighbourhood', including Robert Glen and some of the baillies. It concluded that, 'The dinner and wines fully maintained the well-known reputation of the establishment.'[130]

The population of Linlithgow were well provided for when it came to buying food and drink. Baking and fleshing remained strong at this period. In these days, before refrigeration, supermarkets, out-of-town shopping and packaged or tinned food, there would have been very little importing of foodstuffs into the town. Even so, the sheer number of food and drink outlets in the town at this time seems very striking. Many people had multiple roles, while taverns, grocers, bakers etc. had a surprising degree of overlap. As a result, it is impossible and meaningless to try to calculate the number of people who worked in a particular part of the sector.

---

128   The Glasgow Herald, 20th January 1851
129   The Scotsman, 1st March 1851
130   The Scotsman, 20th March 1851

The Star & Garter Hotel

d. Other Trades

A number of other people gave occupations that indicate that they were involved in retail or commerce within the town. Some are rather unspecific as to what sort of trade they were employed in. In the first instance we will attempt to divide them between employees and employers.

Those who appear to have been employees are made up of four shopkeepers, one shop woman, one apprentice shopkeeper, one mercantile clerk, one merchant's assistant, one general assistant, one errand girl and two errand boys. Most tantalising is the entry for John Thomas who is given as 'Merchant Clerk Glasgow'. There is very little evidence to suggest that people commuted between Linlithgow and the two great cities at either end of the railway line. Perhaps John Thomas did, or perhaps his entry conceals that he was a visitor: he was resident on the night of the census in the house of his brother Alexander, a retired engineer, but is not recorded as being a visitor.

That the shopkeepers were employees rather than small business people is indicated by their absence from Slater. Presumably in the same way that a housekeeper would not be the owner of the house, a shopkeeper kept rather than owned a shop.

One employee that stands out on his own was Andrew H Baird. Born in Muirkirk in Ayrshire, and 22 years old, he was a travelling salesman (possibly the town's first) for a soap manufacturer.

Turning to those who were not employees but traders in their own right, bottom of the pile were the hawkers who sold small bits and pieces door to door and were probably considered to be one step up from paupers. Linlithgow had thirteen of them in 1851. Five had come from Ireland and four from Edinburgh. They were generally an older group with an average age of 46 and only one under 35. The oldest was 80 year old William McNight, an Irish man who lodged at 84 High Street.

What of the others? Sarah Anderson gave little away in giving her occupation as a general merchant. Neither did John McLean, who simply called himself a merchant. Fuel was supplied to the town by James Dodds and David Henderson, coal merchants. The latter was also a magistrate. William Wotherspon dealt in corn while John Pender dealt in grain.

Margaret Duff was a hardware shopkeeper in competition with Janet Bennie, ironmonger, a line of trade that might have been expected to fall to men. Did they import items into the town that the blacksmiths didn't produce?

The residents could eat off the goods provided by Thomas Glen or Humphrey Rutherford (dealers in stoneware), Christina Scott (crockeryware merchant), or Margaret McIntyre (delf merchant[131]). Margaret may well have been the wife of John McIntyre who appears in Slater the following year as an earthenware dealer. Perhaps he was away on business on the night of the census.

To fill their china cups they could visit Peter Roberts (tea dealer and merchant) or James Service (tea and coffee merchant). None of these lines of trade appear in the 1841 census or the 1837 trade directory.

Medicine for the spirit or the body could be purchased from Agnes Waldie, book seller and druggist, who appears to have taken over from her late husband Alexander (died 1846).[132] Books were often published unbound, but if someone

---

131   'Delf' is likely to be a variation on 'Delft'
132   Mitchell & Mitchell, p27

wanted a book to be bound, or rebound, then the person to take it to was Christina Aikenhead, book binder. One wonders what items passed through the hands of auctioneer William Laidlaw.

An advert in The Scotsman for a public auction at Walton farm in which Laidlaw was to preside gives us some idea:

> 'Stock and implements on said farm:
> 6 work horses
> 1 mare and foal
> 1 gig horse, gig and harness
> 6 milch cows
> 5 queys and 5 calves
> 2 stots and 1 bull
> 7 common carts and 4 corn do.
> 1 water do.
> 3 2-horse ploughs and 2 double mould do.
> 1 4-horse grubber and 1 drill do.
> 4 pairs harrows
> 1 metal roller and 1 wooden do.
> 1 turnip sowing machine and 1 bean do.
> Cart and plough harness, small implements, etc, etc, also dairy and kitchen utensils.'[133]

Of this collection of seventeen traders and merchants, nine hailed from Linlithgow and eight were incomers. With an average age of 43 they were among the more mature groups within the working society. It seems likely that the independent, successful women in this group were amongst the most high profile within the town.

One curiosity is Hunter and Co., tobacconists. In the Gazette series of articles in 1901 looking back to 1851 this company is included in the list of traders[134] yet there is no mention of them in Slater and no-one in the 1851 census, Hunter or not, who said they worked as, or for, a tobacconist. Perhaps Mr or Mrs Hunter had died in the early part of 1851 leaving the town without a tobacco supplier. In Pigot, the following year, this role had been filled by a Peter Roberts.

---

133   The Scotsman, 5th November 1851
134   Linlithgowshire Gazette, 3rd May 1901, p6.

Summary

Linlithgow enjoyed a wide range of commercial activity, a range which had expanded since 1841. The town may have lost its tobacconist (temporarily) but had gained a number of new lines. This would appear to have been a decade in which improved transport and affluence had brought a broader choice of goods into the town.

Transport and Communication

a.   Carters and Carriers

Carters or carriers have already been mentioned twice in this book: firstly, under the name of whipmen, in the list of fraternities which had a traditional right to a seat on the council; secondly in connection with the transport of goods to and from the distillery and brewery. Of course, the transportation of goods and materials would have been vital for all the industries within the town, fulfilling the role taken by delivery men with their vans and lorries today.

In 1841 Baillie found 29 carters and carriers within the town at a point just before the arrival of the railway. Ten years later the number had increased slightly to 31. Two offer a little more information about what they were transporting. Isabella Peat, the only woman in the business, was a victuals carrier, while John Finnie was a carter and spirit dealer. Neither appears in Slater as a grocer or spirit dealer so presumably carting was the main aspect of their businesses. Thomas Lesslie gives himself as a carter in the census but in Slater is listed as a hay and straw dealer. Born in Bathgate, in 1851 he was living at the Red Lion with his brother James, the innkeeper.

Carters and carriers were spread throughout the age range from three teenagers up to two men in their seventies. The average age was 36.

Nineteen of the carters and carriers were from Linlithgow parish and nine more were from the rest of West Lothian, showing that this part of the economy was firmly in local hands. Mysteriously, Slater's Trade Directory of 1852 mentions three carriers, James and John Drumbrack and James Johnston, running services to Edinburgh, Glasgow and Bo'ness respectively, yet not one of them appears in West Lothian in the 1851 census. There is a James Johnstone in Bo'ness in1851 who appears as a carrier and may well be our man. As for the Drumbracks, there is no sign of them under any obvious variant spelling: perhaps they lived in Edinburgh and Glasgow.

Who kept the books for the carters? John Christie gave his occupation as carter's clerk. Maybe the rest did it themselves or had a family member to help them.

So much for goods; people also required transportation. There were three coachmen and two coach drivers in the parish. The former appear to have worked at the big houses or farms while the latter lived in town. James Ainslie was a coach proprietor and one of the two coach drivers was his brother Archibald. James may have run the omnibus service recorded in Slater which ran daily (and twice on Wednesdays) to Bathgate from the railway station. Compare this to 1837 when Pigot detailed three passage boats a day to Edinburgh and two to Glasgow as well as four daily coaches to Edinburgh, one to Glasgow and one to Stirling. All these had fallen by the wayside as railway travel had come into the ascendancy.

b.   Postal Service

In an age where technology has made communication across the world almost instantaneous, it can be hard to imagine a time when a letter overseas could take months to arrive, as happened in so many early nineteenth century novels. Even momentous events on the near Continent, such as the Battle of Waterloo, could take days to be known in Britain. The spread of railways speeded up communication around the country, both by physically transporting letters and packages, and also because the railway lines were adopted by an emerging technology, the telegraph, to link major cities with poles being built alongside the tracks. The first long distance telegraph line in Europe was built in 1838 linking London and Birmingham[135] and the first submarine telegraph cable was laid between Britain and France in 1850.[136] In 1847 the Queen's speech at the opening of Parliament was relayed by telegraph to 60 towns and cities across Britain within two hours.[137]

The Penny Post had been introduced across the country in 1840 and in 1843 Andrew Bell reported that there was one Post Office in the parish, based, of

---

135   Prescott, p9
136   Philip's World History Encyclopedia, p495
137   Shipping Gazette & Sydney General Trade List Vol 5; Page 118; 20 May 1848

course, in Linlithgow.[138] Slater details a complex series of arrivals, distributions and dispatches to and from different locations at different times of day from half past seven in the morning until five in the afternoon.

In 1851 we find the Post Office in the hands of Marion Speeden, Post Mistress, assisted by her sister and sister-in-law. The Speedens were not alone in managing the mail: John Martin, who doubled up as a shoemaker, had an undefined role within the Post Office and there were three men who would be called postmen today: two (aged 29 and 36) gave their occupation as 'Post Boy', while there was one 62 year old man who supplemented his naval pension as a 'Letter Carrier'. He was born in Tranent and the elder 'Boy' was born in Ayr: all the rest of the postal workers were born in Linlithgow.

Summary

Within and around the town the horse and cart were still an essential part of the Linlithgow economic machine and would continue to be so for decades to come until motorised transport took their place. For travel outwith the neighbourhood, the success of the railways had led to the demise of passenger transport on the canal and the elimination of most coach routes.

The number of postal workers is testament to the volume of mail being processed at this early date.

Public Service

a.   Civil Servants

Linlithgow was, of course, the county town for West Lothian, or Linlithgowshire. As an administrative centre, it was the work place for a number of people in jobs which we now consider part of the civil service.

Within West Lothian the Inland Revenue had men working in Bathgate (two), Bo'ness (three), Kirkliston (two) and Queensferry (three) but the largest number were in Linlithgow (eight). Of these, six were officers or collectors, one was a clerk and one was the supervisor, William Ridley. This work was not without its

---

138   NSA, p183

moments of excitement. In April 1850 the Glasgow Herald reported a raid, led by Ridley's predecessor, Alexander Fraser, on an illicit still near Bathgate 'within a few hundred yards of the residence of one of our most active county magistrates'.[139]

Interestingly, not one of the eighteen revenue men in West Lothian came from the county. Half of them had come up from England, including three of those in Linlithgow. English tax collectors in Linlithgow – one hopes that they were well received in the community! Another of the Linlithgow group had come even further - Halifax, Nova Scotia. This does not seem to have been a well-settled occupation. Four of the Linlithgow Revenue Officers were living in lodgings. Is this evidence of a national market for this specialised work with staff moving round the country as their careers developed? Not surprisingly they were a mature group with an average age of nearly 44.

As well as the revenue men, there were three excise collectors in the county: one in Bathgate, one in Livingston and 77 year old Alexander Williamson in Linlithgow. Francis Innes, aged 45 and born in the Isle of Wight, was a surveyor of taxes. Finally, there were two toll keepers – James Robertson at the Burghmuir Toll and Thomas Chalmers at Toll Bar House.

One woman could be classed as a 'civil servant': 51 year old Helen McCulloch was the sub 'keeper' at the palace. The title of 'keeper' was usually held by a member of the nobility. By 1851 it may have been the Earl of Hopetoun. The real work would have fallen to Helen. The palace was not being left to decay gently. A parliamentary paper listed expenditure from parliamentary grants on Linlithgow Palace, as well as other buildings. In 1847-8 this amounted to £35, in 1848-9 £34 and in 1849-50 £26.[140]

b.   The Town Council

Turning to the administration of the burgh, up at the top of the tree we find John Hardy, the Provost. Given the degree to which local families controlled key aspects of the town, we might expect to find a local man in this role. While it comes as a surprise, therefore, to find that Hardy was born in Ireland he had in fact spent most of his life in Linlithgow. His father, James, was a sergeant in the Linlithgowshire Yeomanry Cavalry and lies buried in St Michael's churchyard. One may suppose that James was stationed in Ireland at the time of John's birth. John

---

139   *Glasgow Herald, 12th April 1850*
140   *The Scotsman, 5th July 1851*

was a writer (solicitor) and had cut his teeth, professionally speaking, in the office of the Sheriff Clerk in Linlithgow. Having developed his career in Edinburgh (where we worked in the office of Archibald Scott, Procurator Fiscal, during the period of the Burke and Hare trials[141]) he returned to Linlithgow in 1829. From that date onwards, his career went from strength to strength within the town and county. As well as his legal career, Hardy seems to have had a number of other interests. He was the secretary for the Kinneil Races in July 1850[142] and 1851.[143] He seems to have inherited some of his father's interest in the military: for a number of years he was the captain of the No. 1 (Linlithgow) Company of the Linlithgowshire Rifle Volunteers.[144] He was Provost from 1848 to 1855, one of only two members outside the Dawson family to hold the post between 1811 and 1881.

The Dawson dynasty had been started by Adam Dawson, the relocator of the distillery. He had been Provost from 1811 to 1818. His successor was John Boyd, who held office until 1830. Adam Dawson's son, also Adam, had taken up the reins at that point and served until 1848. The second Adam was author of a book in 1868 called 'Rambling Recollections of Past Times' which sheds some interesting light on Linlithgow, Edinburgh and Scotland in the first decades of the nineteenth century. At the bottom of Table 13 we see John Dawson, the distiller resident in Green Park and younger brother of the second Adam. He became provost in 1855 and remained in the post until 1869, when it was taken up by his brother Adam's son. This son was the third Provost Adam Dawson. He was to hold the position until 1881. In this way, four members of the same family, over three generations, held the leading position in the town council for 51 years in a 70 years period.

As noted before, 1851 was the final year of the old 27 member council. The members were listed in the Gazette article 'Linlithgow in 1851'.[145] Almost all of the council members appeared in Slater's Trade Directory the following year and a number of the names come up in other parts of this book:

---

141   West Lothian Courier, 22nd December 1877
142   Caledonian Mercury, 17th June 1850
143   Glasgow Herald, 26th June 1851
144   West Lothian Courier, 22nd December 1877, p2
145   Linlithgowshire Gazette, 12th April 1901, p6

Table 13. Linlithgow Burgh Council members, 1851

Name	Age	Birth Place	Role	1851 Census Occupation
John Hardy	45	Ireland	Provost	Writer
John Landels	56	Berwickshire	Baillie	Builder
William Howison	48	Fife	Baillie	Brewer
David Henderson	53	Linlithgow	Baillie	Coal Merchant
Edward Spence	45	Linlithgow	Baillie	Shoemaker
John Hutton	64	Linlithgow	Treasurer	Grocer
Andrew Mickel	43	Linlithgow	Dean of Guild	Wright
Edward A. Jardine	51	Edinburgh	Councillor	Proprietor of Houses
Edward Morton jun.	44	Linlithgow	Councillor	Baker
A. M. Callander	32	Linlithgow	Councillor	Currier
Archibald Henderson	40	Linlithgow	Councillor	Builder
William Rule	61	Linlithgow	Councillor	Baker & Spirit Dealer
Peter Roberts	35	Linlithgow	Councillor	Tea Dealer & Merchant
John Adams	43	Linlithgow	Councillor	Spirit Merchant
James Hay	41	Haddington	Councillor	Draper
Andrew Ramsay	50	Linlithgow	Councillor	Nurseryman
Alexander Spence	55	Linlithgow	Councillor	Shoemaker
James Law	36	Linlithgow	Councillor	Tanner & Currier
John McElfrish	31	Linlithgow	Councillor	Glue Manufacturer
Robert Aitken	62	Midlothian	Councillor	Joiner
William Law	68	Linlithgow	Councillor	Tanner
John Kirsopp*	44	England	Councillor	Draper
Edward Spence**			Councillor	
Andrew Speeden	48	Linlithgow	Councillor	Currier
Joseph McNiven	45	Crieff	Councillor	Millwright
William Dymock	34	Linlithgow	Councillor	Grocer
John Dawson	52	Linlithgow	Councillor	Distiller

* John Kirsopp became a bailie following the resignation of Edward Spence in January 1851.
** There is only one Edward Spence in the 1851 census and in Slater's Directory. The second entry of the same name in the list would appear to be an error.

Linlithgow born men made up about two thirds of the members. It is clear that the mediaeval system had broken down as a number of trades were not represented. In fact of the fifteen incorporated trades and fraternities, eight had no representative amongst these men: the smiths, tailors, weavers, coopers, fleshers, dyers, hecklers and whipmen. Of these, the weavers, dyers, hecklers and whipmen also failed to make it into the 1837 or 1852 trade directories.

The Town Clerk was Robert R Glen, a writer, and a man who crops up in many places in this book. Keeping order was Adam Colquhoun, superintendent of the police within the county and a Justice of the Peace.

There were two Burgh Officers who would have worked in the administration of the burgh. Two men (father and son George and Alexander Graham) are recorded with the strange occupation of 'collector of burgh clattern'. This is an unusual term: fortunately George has an entry in Slater's Directory as 'collector of towns customs, West Port', which clarifies the role.

Finally, in this category, there is one lady to be mentioned: 73 year old Jane Jack was the Keeper of the County Buildings.

Professions

a.   Legal

The law touched on many aspects of life in 1851, just as it does today. The number of people within the town who were involved with the law was boosted by the presence of the county court and the county prison.

For day-to-day activities, such as buying and selling property and dealing with wills, the populace needed the services of writers, as solicitors were known.

	Writers	Notaries
Pigot's Trade Directory (1837)	6	3
Slater's Trade Directory (1852)	6	4

John Cay, Sheriff of Linlithgow. Photograph by Hill and Adamson. Cay was not prsent in Linlithgow on the night of the census. Courtesy of Glasgow University Library, Department of Special Collections.

The importance of these men is clear from their other activities. We have already seen that John Hardy was the provost: he was also a clerk of the peace, and commissioner for the burgh on a number of boards. Under Agriculture, we saw Robert Glen advertising for a new tenant for Pardovan farm, and under Food and Drink we saw him acting in the letting of the Star and Garter. His entry in Slater's list of 1852 describes him as a writer 'and town clerk, treasurer for the county and clerk to the commissioners of supply, to the rural police committee, and to the prison board'.[146] We will see under 'Financial' that he was also a local bank manager. In fact all six of the men listed in Slater as writers give different descriptions of their occupations in the 1851 census. Thomas Dick and James Roberts gave themselves as 'Procurators of the Sheriff Court'. Peter Miller was a 'Writer in the Sheriff Court'. James Watson was Procurator Fiscal with a salary of 12 guineas.[147]

---

146   *Slater's Directory, p775*
147   *Linlithgowshire Gazette, 12th April 1901, p6*

Grand Match at Linlithgow, 1848.

Two Linlithgow men, Robert Glen and Adam Dawson (second provost of that name) are shown in this painting by Charles Lees of the 'Grand Match at Linlithgow 1848'. It portrays 47 notable curlers who were present at the event, held on the 25th January that year. In total 280 competitors took part, representing either 'the north' or 'the south'. The list of names in the key diagram shows the elevated company in which Glen and Dawson mixed.

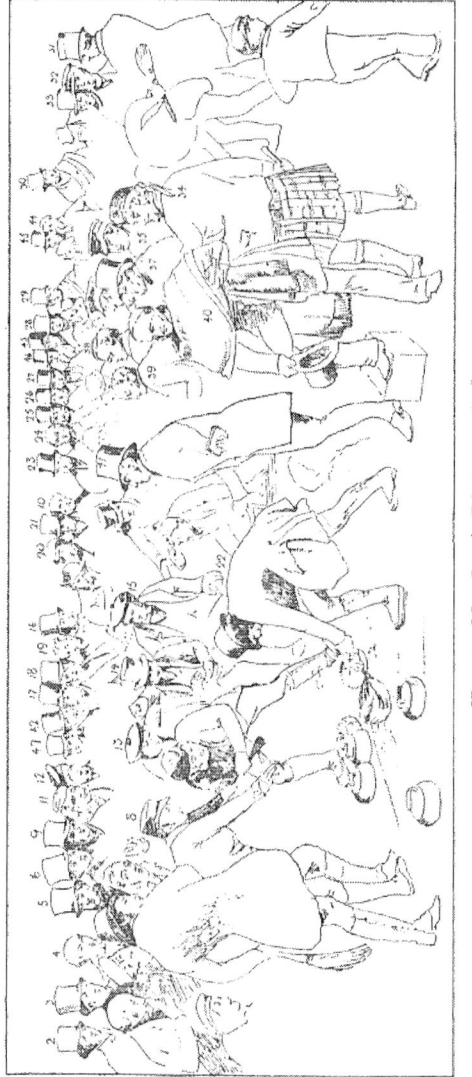

Key to Mr Lees' Picture of the

ROYAL CALEDONIAN CURLING CLUB GRAND MATCH AT LINLITHGOW.

1. Sir George Clerk, Bt., of Penicuick.
2. Rev. A. L. Simpson, D.D., Kirknewton
3. Sir W. Gibson-Craig, Bt., of Riccarton
4. Col. Dundas, of Carronhall.
5. Sir Patk. Murray Thriepland.
6. The Right Hon. Lord Kinnaird
7. C. Cowan, Esq., of Valleyfield, M.P.
8. Robert Palmer, Esq., Currie.
9. Allan Pollok, Esq., of Broom.
10. Arthur Pollok, Esq.
11. Major Henderson, of Westerton.
12. Col. M'Dowall of Garthland.
13. Mr Piper.
14. T. Durham Weir, Esq., of Boghead.
15. J. Moore, Esq., Solicitor, Edinburgh.
16. F. S. Wedderburn, Esq., of Wedderburn.

17. Capt. H. Maitland-Dougall, of Scots-craig.
18. Col. Low, Cairnie Lodge.
19. D. Gillespie, Esq., of Mountquhanie.
20. Wm. Horsburgh, Esq., Cupar-Fife.
21. Thomas Anderson, Esq., Newburgh.
22. Mr John M'George, late Medalist.
23. Archd. Thomson, Esq., Edinburgh.
24. Alex. Russel, Esq., Edinburgh.
25. W. Dumbreck, Esq., M.D., Edinr.
26. John Haig, Esq., Cameron Bridge.
27. J. W. Williamson, Esq., Kinross.
28. John Cunningham, Esq., Edinburgh.
29. W. Wilson, Esq., of Water Meetings.
30. Robert Moubray, Esq., of Cambus.
31. Andrew Gillon, Esq., of Wallhouse.
32. Robert R. Glen, Esq., Linlithgow.

33. Adam Dawson, Esq., of Bonnytown.
34. His Grace the Duke of Athole.
35. J. Murray Drummond, Esq. of Megginch.
36. David Wylie, Esq., Edinburgh.
37. Jas. Baird, Esq., of Gartsherrie, M.P.
38. R. B. W. Ramsay, Esq., of Whitehill.
39. Sir John Ogilvy, Bt., of Inverquharity
40. Alex. Cassels, Esq., W.S., Secretary, Royal Club.
41. J. Ogilvie Dalgleish, Esq., of Woodburne.
42. Provost Philips, of Paisley.
43. George Gillespie, Esq., Glasgow.
44. John T. Renton, Esq., London.
45. Charles Elder M'Ritchie, Esq.
46. William I Anson, Esq.
47. Robert Craig, Esq.

We have noted that John Hardy was born in Ireland, though he had lived most of his life in Linlithgow. Peter Miller was born in Perthshire but the other four writers were born in Linlithgow parish. In addition to the six listed in Slater there were two other men in the parish who are recorded as writers in the 1851 census: James C Bauchop was a Writer to the Signet[148] while James Thom was a writer and insurance agent.

Working for the writers as apprentices were eight young men (seven of whom were local) aged fifteen to seventeen and eight clerks (five from Linlithgow). At the Sheriff Court worked Francis Horne (an advocate and sheriff substitute), a messenger-at-arms (responsible for serving documents and enforcing court orders), two Sheriff Officers and two clerks, one of whom was also treasurer of the Subscription Reading Room at the Town Hall. In 1843 Andrew Bell had reported a library left by a Dr Henry and a news-room in the town, as well as a subscription library in Linlithgow Bridge. Neither the census data nor Slater gives any further indication as to their status in 1851.

A number of the legal roles were held by people who had other forms of employment. Two members of the town council were the magistrates: David Henderson, coal merchant, and John Kirsopp, draper. There were four justices of the peace. Two of them were father and son, Adam Dawson senior and junior of Huntburn. At 21 Adam junior was by far the youngest man to be so honoured. In 1869 he would follow in the family tradition and become Provost.

The legal profession was strong within Linlithgow. Its main practitioners were important men within the parish. It was dominated by local men and a new generation of locals was in training. As with retail, those involved in the legal profession seem prone to having many roles.

The county court was a small employer but a significant institution.

b.   County Prison

The county prison was staffed by four people, three of whom also lived there. The governor was 55 year old, Wigan born, James Ellison (who we saw earlier giving up his time to instruct a choir of young people). His wife Susannah, aged 45 from Norfolk, was the matron. The third was Anne Carmichael, 22, from Blackness, who

---

148   *The Society of Writers to Her Majesty's Signet is a society of Scottish solici-*
       tors. Dating back to 1594 it is one of the oldest legal societies in the world.

was a servant. Mr and Mrs Ellison are the same couple who Andrew Bell gave, under the name of Alison, as being in charge of the prison in 1843. Black, in 'The Surnames of Scotland', quotes several sources which state that Alison and Ellison, as well as other variations such as Allinson, were treated as interchangeable.[149] The Wigan and Norfolk accents may not have helped clarify the difference to Scottish ears. In any event, they were recorded as Ellison in the 1841 census.

At the time of the census the Ellisons were being visited by fourteen year old Julia Tooke. Like Susannah she was from Norfolk so may have been a relation. The fourth person who worked at the prison was Adam Stanners, also from England. He was the prison warder. Unlike the Ellisons he did not live there. He and his family lived at 285 High Street.

Comparative Data for Prisoners

1841 Census	12
1851 Census	19

On the night of the census there were 21 inmates in the prison, nineteen adults and two infant girls with their mothers. The census gives no indication as to how long they were in for and what they had done. However, we can report that eight were Irish (five women and three men), there were four from other parts of West Lothian (two women and two men), two from England (a woman and a man), two men each from Perth and Lanarkshire and one man from Linlithgow. That made eleven men and eight women. In these days there was no concept of separate male and female prisons.

Each has their pre-prison occupation recorded against them. From this we can tell that ten of the prisoners were labourers of some sort (general, agricultural and mining) and two were wives of labourers. The others were from a variety of backgrounds, including the only watchmaker to be found in the parish. The age spread of the prisoners was from seventeen to 63 and the average was 32.

Not all the adults in the prison were necessarily convicts. The following notice was placed by James Watson, Procurator Fiscal, in the Caledonian Mercury in July 1851:

'JOAN SIMPSON, residing with JAMES BRUCE, Pensioner, residing at Woodside,

---

149   Black, p18

*in the Parish of Torphichen, and County of Linlithgow, having been committed
to the Prison of Linlithgow for safe custody, as being a Lunatic, intimation is
made that the Sheriff will, at Twelve o'Clock Noon of Monday the 28th day of
July current, in the Ordinary Sheriff-Court Room, Linlithgow, proceed to take
evidence of the condition of the said JOAN SIMPSON, as being furious, fatuous,[150]
or a lunatic and dangerous, in terms of the Act of Parliament 4th and 5th
Victoria, chapter 60, intituled "An Act to alter and amend certain Acts regarding
Madhouses in Scotland, and to provide for the custody of dangerous Lunatics."[151]*

Prisoners could also (as now) be held at the prison whilst awaiting trial. In 1856
The Glasgow Herald reported a 'Frightful Murder Near Bathgate'.[152] On the night
of Saturday 15th or Sunday 16th November the Maxwell brothers, Thomas and
John, were ambushed near Durhamtown, just outside Bathgate, by William
Mansfield, Peter McLean and McLean's wife Christine and step-daughter Jane (the
former of which ladies, the paper suggests, may have taken part in the attack).
McLean had purchased a knife prior to leaving Bathgate that evening, intent
on murdering John Maxwell 'with whom he has had some difference regarding
their views of religion'.[153] They got the wrong man: John was injured but Thomas
was killed. Two policemen from Bathgate were alerted and forced their way into
the house of the attackers where they found them 'in the very act of washing
the blood from their hands'.[154] The accused were held in Linlithgow Prison until
evidence could be gathered to 'prevent the perpetrators of such a horrible deed
escaping punishment.' It sounds as if the press had already reached a guilty
verdict!

The following January Peter McLean was found guilty and three weeks later he
was hung. To the end he maintained that if he had committed the crime he had
no memory of it, while his wife, somewhat contradictorily, argued that 'There is
no doubt that Peter was guilty; but Mansfield was as bad as him, and should have
got the same sentence.'[155]

It would seem that there was concern over the size of the facilities. The following
advert appeared in The Scotsman in September 1851:

---

150 *In the 19th century 'fatuous' would have meant an imbecile or simpleton.*
151 *Caledonian Mercury, 21st July 1851*
152 *Glasgow Herald, 21st November 1856*
153 *The Caledonian Mercury adds that the Maxwells were Irish Catholics and
     their attackers were Irish Protestants.*
154 *Glasgow Herald, 21st November 1856*
155 *Glasgow Herald, 5th February 1857*

'Wanted immediately, estimates for building an extension of the county prison of Linlithgow. The plans and specifications will be seen in the hands of Messrs Brown and Wardrop, architects, 19 St Andrew Square, Edinburgh – by whom, or Mr Glen, Clerk to the County Prison Board at Linlithgow, Tenders will be received till the 12th of September 1851.[156]

Why use outside architects? No-one in Linlithgow laid claim to that profession in either the census of Slater.

c.   Financial

Under Agriculture we saw Mr Glen's advert for Pardovan Farm in which part payment in grain was suggested. Despite this it appears that Linlithgow had a very money based economy. In 1837 Pigot had reported one bank, the Commercial Bank of Scotland. By 1852 Slater records that an additional bank was in operation: the Western Bank of Scotland. The Western had grown rapidly through the 1830s and 40s, absorbing a number of the local banks that were springing up across the country in a series of takeovers and mergers. At its height, it was the second largest bank in Scotland, behind only the Royal Bank. Throughout this period, the Western had a reputation for sailing close to the wind and it was to collapse in spectacular fashion in 1857. It had invested heavily in North America and when a series of bankruptcies hit New York the rottenness of the Western's balance sheet became apparent. With nervous Scottish depositors wanting their money back it became clear that the bank had been lending freely but keeping little back by way of reserves. Within two months its doors were shut.

Returning to 1851, the two bank branch managers were men already mentioned in this work. The Commercial was run by Robert Riddoch Glen, writer, town clerk, sometime farmer and clerk or treasurer to too many bodies to mention, including the County Prison Board. The Western was run by Adam Dawson, scion of the Huntburn Dawsons and at 21 the youngest Justice of the Peace in the parish.

Under them worked two accountants, one clerk and one apprentice clerk. Although the two principals were local men most of the rest were incomers, one of the accountants being the only exception.

For those for whom banking was not the answer to their monetary needs, Charles

---

156   *The Scotsman, 3rd September 1851*

McKay, 45, from Ireland, ran the county's only pawnbrokers. Pawnbroking was sufficiently prestigious to merit an entry in Slater's Trade Directory. The McKays lived in 254 High Street. They had a servant, an Irish woman called Sarah Cussick, and three small children. Living with them were Charles's brother (railway labourer), his nephew (a scholar) and his brother-in-law (a tailor). The house must have been busy on the night of the census as they were also entertaining four visitors.

Banking was on the increase and men like Robert Glen had a part to play in many major transactions. Once again, the Dawsons were involved in an important aspect of the town's economy.

d.   Education

Comparative Data for Schools

	Schools	Individual Teachers
1837 Pigot	4	1
1852 Slater	5	5*

* Four in Linlithgow and a fifth in Linlithgow Bridge under Thomas Marshall.

We have already seen that Linlithgow had a young population and that many of them (923) were expected at school according to the census. Obviously, all these scholars required a group of teachers to teach them.

Under the heading of 'Academies and Schools' the trade directories list schools (with their rector and master or mistress) and individual educators. It is not clear how the individuals fitted into the education system. However, where they can be identified within the 1851 census they all give their occupation as teacher (sometimes with subject) or, in one case, as governess. It seems likely that the individuals acted as tutors either for groups or individuals.

The main school, a predecessor of the Academy, was known at that time as the Grammar School. In 1851 the rector was William Sheils, aged 30 from Edinburgh. He was paid a salary of £30 with a 'free school house and garden and seat in church.'[157] Additionally, the Douglas Charity School, recorded in the New Statistical Account of 1843, was still in operation under the leadership of Jane Dickson. Helen Heiton was mistress of the Infants' School. There were two

---

157 *Linlithgow Gazette, 12th April 1901, p6.*

schools for dissenters from the Church of Scotland: the Free Church School and the Secessional School. There was no Catholic School at this time.

Some of these schools may have been one man or woman bands and some may have had additional staff. Certainly, from the 1851 census, beyond those named in Slater, there are four teachers, one assistant teacher and two seventeen year old pupil teachers. It seems likely that those last two worked at the Grammar School. Subjects listed in the census entries as being taught by the teachers included reading, writing, arithmetic, English, classics, Latin, French, mercantile, geography and music.

In total, seventeen people were teachers. Only four of them were born in Linlithgow, of whom two were the pupil teachers. The others came from a wide range of places: Midlothian is notable for having provided five. Even excluding the two seventeen year olds the average age of the teachers was quite young at 32. One of the reasons for this may have been that seven of them were women, all of whom were single. The tradition that teaching was a fine occupation for women until they were married continued until well after the Second World War. There were two pairs of sisters in this group. Grace and Elizabeth Cochran were both described simply as teachers while Jessie and Maria Bauchop were both teachers of French and music. Given that Bauchop was a rare name they may have been the daughters of James C Bauchop, writer to the signet, mentioned under Legal.

Charles William Maxwell Muller, 29, who gave his occupation as 'Professor of Music', is not included in the above total. As well as performing, he may have taught and/or had a position with St Michael's Church. Certainly, he appears in Slater under the 'Miscellaneous' notables rather than under 'Academies and Schools'.

Apart from their exotic name, the birthplaces of the Maxwell Mullers make for interesting reading. He was born in Dumfries and was married to Janet, 28, born in Glasgow. Their three children were Eliza, five, born in France, Caroline, three, born in Sardinia, Robert, one, born in Linlithgow, and an unnamed infant also born in Linlithgow. A remarkably well travelled family! Janet herself was a land and house proprietor: which houses and land is not made clear. All that can be said is that they had two servants but no lodgers at their house at 80 High Street on the night of the census.

The family's travels were to continue within Scotland. Through the birth records of their later children, we know that the Maxwell Mullers were in Peebles by 1854, Edinburgh by 1859 and Glasgow by 1862.[158]

Music and travel seem to have run in the family. Charles' baptism entry in the Dumfries Old Parish Records shows that his father, Christian Miller was a musician though when Charles died in 1894, by then a landed gentleman, his father was recorded as Johnann Christoph Muller, professor of music. It seems very likely that Christian/Christoph had come from Germany.

e.   Religion

Image above: St Michael's Parish Church – south view. Engraving by J. H. Le Keux from a drawing by R. W. Billings thought to date to the 1850s. Note the absence of the spire.

Comparative Data for Places of Worship

Pigot's Trade Directory (1837)	4
New Statistical Account (1843)	4
Slater's Trade Directory (1852)	5

---

158   *I am indebted to Robert D. Selbie, great-great-grandson of Charles William and Janet, for information on their later children.*

Eight years after the secession of the Free Church of Scotland the opportunities for religious expression had increased slightly. As well as the Church of Scotland at St Michael's, still in the hands of Andrew Bell, there were two United Secession Churches, a Free Church and an Independent Church. The five churches needed five ministers, and in fact at St Michael's there was even a young probationer assisting Andrew Bell.

The ministers were a surprisingly young bunch with an average age of just under 36. We have already seen that Andrew Bell came from St Andrews. It is notable that not one of the ministers came from Linlithgow or even from West Lothian. Perhaps the need to go to university to qualify as a minister then find oneself a parish acted to break local ties. In fact they came from all round the country: Stow, Tarbolton, Roxburghshire, Aberdeenshire and Nairn.

It may be observed that there was no Catholic church despite the large number of Irish people in the parish. Though there was greater religious tolerance than there had been a century before this was still a thorny issue. It was not until 1793 that the Catholics had regained the right to vote and not until 1829 that they had been permitted to sit in Parliament. In 1851 the town magistrates decided to accept a petition to use the town hall for Catholic worship on every second Sunday. This proved short-lived as the ruling was quickly challenged and overturned by the full council.[159] The strength of the local feelings towards the Catholic Church is shown in a petition that the newly elected MP, Mr Baird, delivered to parliament on Monday 5th May, on behalf of the Congregational Church of Linlithgow, no doubt without any intentional irony:

> '...against Papal aggression, praying that all grants of money may be withdrawn from the Romish institutions, that no diplomatic relations be instituted between this country and the Court of Rome, and that measures be adopted for securing to her Majesty's subjects the same religious toleration in Catholic countries that Catholics enjoy in this country.'[160]

In addition to the ministers the town had a missionary – Adam Gordon, 41, from Sutherland. A missionary was the minister of a small congregation that did not have full congregation status. The birth places of his children suggest that he had been in Lochgilphead from 1840 (or earlier) until around 1845, followed by spells in Oban and Old Kilpatrick. He had been in Linlithgow for at most two

---

159   Linlithgowshire Gazette, 12th April 1901, p6
160   The Morning Chronicle, 6th May 1851

years. How long did he stay here? If he was still in the town in 1852 he was not considered to be one of the 'Gentry and Clergy', as all the ministers were, as he was not included in Slater's Directory. One lady with a clerical connection who did make it into that section of Slater was Mrs Janet Knowles of Rose Bank. She was the widow of Reverend Alexander Knowles, of the Independent Church in Rose Lane, who had died in 1849 'in the 43rd year of ministry'.[161] She was to live on until 1871.

Though none of the ministers on the date of the census were born locally this was to change later in the year. On the 19th February 1851 The Scotsman reported the unanimous selection of John Dobie, son of the late Dr. James Dobie, as the new minister of the West United Presbyterian Church.[162] He returned to the town to take up the position later in the year.

Education and religion were major elements in Linlithgow society with a variety of routes to learning or religious expression available. Teaching and ministering do not seem to have been in the psyche of the local inhabitants, or perhaps locals who followed these paths found that they had led them to other parts of the country. Almost all educators had come into the parish from other areas, notably Midlothian, while all the ministers were incomers from a wide variety of locations.

e.   Medical/Health Care

Comparative Data for Medical Men

	Doctors & Surgeons	Veterinary Surgeons
Pigot's Trade Directory (1837)	3	1
1841 Census	3	1
1851 Census	2	2
Slater's Trade Directory (1852)	2	1

Dealing with animals first, Alexander Nimmo had been the town's veterinary surgeon since at least 1837. Aged 48 in 1851, he had been joined in practice by his twenty year old son Andrew. Alexander was to live to a ripe old age. On his gravestone at St Michael's he is given as having passed away in 1893 aged 90.[163]

The town GP was George Baird, 44, who lived at 5 The Cross. The surgeon was a

161 *Mitchell & Mitchell, p24*
162 *The Scotsman, 19th February 1851, p3*
163 *Mitchell & Mitchell, p28*

27 year old Irishman called Andrew Gilmour. Not surprisingly the other health related roles also went down gender lines: the three midwifes and two nurses were all women. In total there were therefore nine people working directly in healthcare. Other than Andrew Gilmour all the men came from Linlithgow while all the women were incomers. The midwifes were a particularly mature group with an average age of 58. No doubt their experience was much valued by the expectant of the parish.

Despite the increasing population, the level of healthcare provision does not appear to have altered much over the period from 1837 to 1851. Whilst the town seems to have produced its own doctors and vets there does not seem to have been any tradition of nursing or midwifery at this time amongst Linlithgow's women.

Others

a.   Housing

Owning one's own house was much less common in mid nineteenth Century Britain than it is today. Many people could only afford to rent accommodation and a significant minority could only afford a room in a lodging house.

Within Linlithgow in 1851 there seem to have been two categories of people who earned money from housing. Eight women and three men were proprietors of houses, or sometimes of land and houses (such as the previously mentioned Janet Maxwell Muller). These people appear to have rented out flats or houses. Some may have been people who had put their lifesavings into property, or had inherited it, and were living from the income. Other than 28 year old Janet, they were aged between 40 and 80. Even including her, their average age was 62. It was very rare, though not entirely unknown, for people in this group to actually have lodgers in their own house. Only two of the house proprietors came from Linlithgow. There is no clear pattern in the origins of the others.

It is clear that there was already a national market in rented property, at least for the better class of accommodation, with the notices pages of the major Scottish newspapers featuring many 'to let' adverts. For example, from the pages of the Glasgow Herald, in between similar items for properties near Callander and Arran, we find:

'TO LET, FURNISHED
For Three or Four Months, from 1st June

THE VILLA of FRIAR BANK, within a few minutes' walk of the Linlithgow Railroad
Station, consisting of Dining Room, Drawing Room, Parlour, Library, Two
Bed Rooms, and Bed Room Closet &c., with Half an Acre of Ground laid out in
Shrubbery and Garden.
Apply to Capt. Ferguson, Friar Bank, Linlithgow
April 21, 1849' [164]

Lodging house keepers, or lodger keepers, formed the second and larger group. Unlike the house proprietors, the twenty six lodging house keepers habitually shared their own accommodation with their customers. Baillie noted eight lodging house keepers in the town in 1841 and concluded that only one remained after the construction of the railway.[165] It would therefore appear that in the mid to late 1840s the demand for lodgings had greatly increased after a short, sharp decline.

All the lodging house or lodger keepers were women and half of them were Irish. Many of the lodgers were Irish, especially in the establishments run by the Irish women. We have already noted that in 1851 there was a substantial population of low skilled Irish people in Linlithgow, many earning a living working on the railways or in other labouring occupations. Low wages and the unpredictable nature of labouring work would have made living in lodgings the best, or perhaps only, option.

The age profiles of the Irish and non-Irish women in this sector were very similar. In both cases the average age was 53. Of the thirteen non-Irish women, five came from Linlithgow, two from other parts of West Lothian, three from Stirlingshire, one from Midlothian, one from Fife and one from Thurso in Caithness.

Demand for rented accommodation in Linlithgow was high. House proprietors were mostly men and mostly quite old. The itinerant, or low paid, incomers often found somewhere to live in lodging houses, all of which were run by women. Elements of the Irish community had found a way of earning a living taking in lodgers, many of whom were also Irish.

---

164   *Glasgow Herald, 23rd April 1849*
165   *Baillie, p26*

## b.	Hair Care

The town's only barber was a man. This was Robert Shields, now 51, who had been cutting the town's hair since at least 1837, given his entry in Pigot. Though recording his occupation as a barber in the census he was listed as a hairdresser in both of the trade directories.

## c.	Forester

There were 36 foresters in West Lothian in 1851 but only one in the parish of Linlithgow. He was William Stevenson, aged seventeen, born in Torphichen but living with his uncle at 111 High Street. Almost half the foresters in the county lived in neighbouring Abercorn. It is just possible that William worked in Abercorn – he wouldn't find much work in his line in the High Street.

## d.	The Arts

Two men remain to be recorded and they could both be categorised as falling under the banner of arts. James Muline, aged 50 from Ireland, was a musician while James Stein, aged 70 from Clackmannanshire was the only artist not just in the parish but the whole county. He lived with his daughter, Mary McKenzie Stein, who is discussed under English Women in Chapter 5. He seems to have specialised as a landscape painter. The Scotsman records a number of sales of his work, for what were substantial sums of money, through the 1840s including: 'View on the Teith' (£12), 'Loch Vennacher' (£15), 'Doune Castle' (£10), 'Cottages in Kinross-shire' (£7), 'Mill Dam on the Tyne' (£30) and 'Study of trees near Coldstream'. His 'Glenfinlas' was described by The Scotsman in 1860 as 'harmonious in colour and tone'.[166]

Unfortunately it is not clear exactly how James Muline made his living.

At least part of the activities of Charles William Maxwell Muller, Professor of Music, should appear under this category. We saw him earlier performing in the musical event at the St Michael's in June 1851.

166	*The Scotsman, 13th March 1860*

Employment Summary

Figures include all staff involved in a trade or sector, not just the skilled craftspeople.

Table 14 Employment on Linlithgow as shown in 1851 Census

Occupation/Sector	Male	Female	Total
Related to Leather			
Shoemaking	326	14	340
Tanning	20	0	20
Currying	43	0	43
Glue Making	23	0	23
Saddlers	9	0	9
Agriculture	**384**	**100**	**484**
Railways	**270**	**0**	**270**
Quarrying & Mining	**63**	**0**	**63**
General Labourers	**94**	**0**	**94**
Forester	**1**	**0**	**1**
Servants/Helping Hands			
Domestic	20	436	456
Gardeners	19	0	19
Laundry	0	14	14
Textile Related			
Calico Manufacture	64	90	154
Tambourers	0	48	48
Weavers	8	0	8
Dressmakers	0	49	49
Hat/Bonnet Makers	0	7	7
Tailors	24	0	24
Drapers	9	2	11
Building Trades			
Masons	60	0	90
Slaters	9	0	9

House Painters	7	0	7
Plasterers	3	0	3
Plumber	1	0	1
Carpenters/Joiners/Wrights	59	0	59
Other woodworkers	8	0	7
Blacksmiths	34	0	34
Other metalworkers	5	0	0
Engineers	5	0	5
Brewing			
Maltsters	8	0	8
Labourers	9	0	9
Coopers	5	0	5
Others	8	0	3
Paper Making			
Paper Makers	8	0	8
Others	10	35	45
Other Manufacture			
Rope Makers	3	0	3
Basket Maker	1	0	1
Soap Maker*	1	0	1
Candle Making	1	0	1
Commerce			
Bakers	43	1	44
Fleshers (butchers)	14	1	15
Grocers/Spirits/Victuals	28	26	54
Pubs and Hotels	10	4	14
Other Trade/Retail	28	16	44
Transport & Communication			
Carter & Carriers	30	1	31
Coachmen/drivers	5	0	5
Postal service	4	3	7
Canals	3	0	3
Roads	1	0	1

Civil Servants			
Inland Revenue	8	0	8
Other tax/toll/customs	6	0	6
Burgh Officers	2	0	2
Building keepers	0	2	2
Legal	**32**	**0**	**32**
County Prison	**2**	**1**	**3**
Finance	**6**	**0**	**6**
Education	**10**	**7**	**17**
Professor of Music	1	0	1
Religion	**7**	**0**	**7**
Medical/Health Care	**4**	**5**	**9**
Housing			
House Proprietors	3	8	11
Lodging Houses	0	26	26
The Arts	**2**	**0**	**2**
Barber/Hairdresser	**1**	**0**	**1**

*Soap was also made as a by-product by glue manufacturers

CHAPTER FOUR
EMPLOYMENT
BY PLACE OF BIRTH

Tables 17-19 in the Appendix split the 1851 populace up by place of birth. In this chapter we will consider the employment profiles of the areas which provided the largest number of people to Linlithgow parish.

Employment levels were very high for men and almost all can be categorised. As already noted, employment amongst women was much lower than men. The high majority of these women seem to have been supported or self-supporting. In this category all those have been included for whom no occupation was stated, those who were described as 'At Home', those who were independently wealthy, those who were land or property owners and those who are described in terms of their relationship to the head of the house. A much smaller proportion were paupers and therefore dependent on state or charitable support.

Place of Birth: Linlithgow

We have already seen that just over half of the population (52.5%) were born in the parish. However, because a much higher proportion of the children were born in Linlithgow the proportion of natives amongst the working age population (13+) was somewhat lower at 43.5%.

a.   Men

Men in Linlithgow were most likely to be employed in the apprenticed trades. Shoemaking was by far the largest employer of local men, to which could be added the related leather trades, the construction trades (other than the masons) and baking. Indeed, looking back at the list of incorporated trades which had sat on the old burgh council before it was reformed, we find Linlithgow born men in disproportionately high numbers across the board:

Table 15. Linlithgow men employed in traditional trades

	Linlithgow Born	Percentage of all men rmployed in the trade
Incorporated Trades		
Shoemakers	255	78.0%
Bakers*	28	65.1%
Smiths	18	59.4%
Wrights	12	66.7%
Tailors	11	47.8%
Weavers	9	75.0%
Fleshers	7	50.0%
Coopers	3	60.0%

* *The figures are 29 and 65.9% if Isabella Duncan, the town's only female baker is included.*

The figures are generally higher for those at the tops of the trades, the masters or those whose names appear in Pigot, and amongst the apprentices. Many of the incomers were journeymen. The figures for the related leather trades are even higher: 80% of tanners, 84% of curriers and 87% of glue makers came from the town.

Table 15 also makes it clear which of the traditional trades were in decline. Handloom weavers were on the verge of becoming an anachronism while the coopers had almost been eliminated. Considering that distilling, brewing and other manufacture in the town still required the production of barrels this suggests that the trade was succumbing to imports from more efficient centres.

Men born in Linlithgow were much less likely than average to be working in occupations with a high labouring component. The local born contingent makes up around a third of agriculture, mining and general labourers. The first two of these groups, obviously, involved working outwith the town while the third was flexible. Two outlets for unskilled young men within the broader town beyond the burgh boundary (including Linlithgow Bridge) were the paper mill and the calico printfield. The latter, in particular, employed many of the youngest workers in the parish. Both of these operations had a mix of unskilled and skilled labour and we have seen that two thirds of the calico printers were locals. The Linlithgow male involvement amounted to 42% at the paper mill and 48% at the printfield. Only one Linlithgow man was a railway labourer.

As the county town, Linlithgow supported a disproportionate number of professional men. In general these men were incomers to the town. The one area of professional life which Linlithgow men had taken a strong grip of was the law: 66% of the legal men in the parish were born there. A similar percentage of local men sat on the burgh council while both of the town's two bank managers were locals. These were, of course, crucial elements of local life, at the heart of the major events and institutions of the town.

b.   Women

Just over half of the women born in Linlithgow did not take part in the formal labour force: 48% fell into the categories that suggest that they were supported or self-supporting and thus did not need to have a formal job. Of course many of them may have worked occasionally or informally. Some were not so fortunate: 4% were paupers, and had to rely on state charity to support them. The proportion of paupers is higher than for other incomers. Two likely reasons for this are that paupers lacked the money to travel, and that they were not made terribly welcome if they did: parishes were much happier to support their own poor than incomers.

Linlithgow born girls were much more likely to stay in school after their twelfth birthday than those who had moved into the parish. Of the 51 girl scholars aged thirteen or over, 42 of them were locals. Incoming girls could, of course, arrive at any age from infancy onwards and the census data does not always make it clear how long they had been in Linlithgow. For older arrivals, the mere fact of emigration could have spelt an end to their schooling. Of course, all the girls did leave school eventually, at which point many of them needed to find a job.

The opportunities that existed for skilled employment were much more restricted for women than for men. Keeping in mind that 43.5% of the adult population came from the parish, Linlithgow women were under-represented in the main female employment area (see Table 6). Although 146 Linlithgow women were servants they only made up a third of the total. They did, however, make up a higher proportion of the more senior roles: sixteen of the 34 (47%) housekeepers were born in the parish. In contrast the next biggest employment group, textiles, was dominated by Linlithgow women: 87 of them worked at the calico printfield giving them 82% of the female workers in that industry. Nearly 90% of the tambourers were locals as were 55% of dressmakers and 63% of seamstresses.

Of course, a sizeable number of women worked in agriculture. While there were fewer female then male agricultural labourers, Table 6 shows that it was the second largest area of employment for women: 35 of them were locals. As with the men, this meant that local women were employed in this sector in disproportionately low numbers. To the 35 must, of course, be added the wives and daughters whose contribution to the farms they lived on is unrecorded by the census.

The main sector in which women could build a career was business. While many were employed by retailers or merchants, a significant proportion owned their own business. A total of 47 women were involved in businesses in one capacity or another and 30 (64%) of them were born in the parish. Coincidentally, and at the lower end of the economy, 64% was also the proportion of washer and mangle women who were locally born.

While women were generally excluded from the apprenticed trades, there were some who managed to have an involvement and the bulk of these were local women. In shoemaking, fourteen women were boot and shoe binders and eleven of them were local. As noted above, the town's only female baker was born in the town.

Summary

Linlithgow men were most likely to be involved in the traditional skilled trades, where these had not been overtaken by advances elsewhere. Linlithgow men were much less likely than incomers to be employed in labouring or unskilled jobs. The only professional area in the grip of Linlithgow men was the law and banking. They also dominated the council.

Linlithgow women, if they worked, were most likely to be servants. However, the employment areas in which they were most dominant were textiles and in the town's shops and other businesses. The dying art of tambouring was largely in their hands. Young women who might have become tambourers in decades gone by now worked in calico printing or dressmaking. Outside the town a number of local women worked in agriculture but in lower proportions than incomers.

Place of Birth: The Rest of West Lothian

West Lothian incomers

	All	Aged 13+	Aged 0-12
Men	268	211	57
Women	380	304	76
Total	648	515	133

Of all incomers to the parish, those from the rest of West Lothian had the smallest, and in some ways the most obvious, journey to make. For most parts of the parish, Linlithgow was the urban centre to which they had the best transportation links, at least until the opening of the railway from Edinburgh to Bathgate in 1848. As the county town, it would also be a place to which many of them travelled from time to time for business or pleasure. In the 1851 census, we find 380 female (304 aged thirteen or over) and 268 male (211 aged thirteen or over) incomers from the other parishes. Table 17 shows that Bo'ness, Kirkliston, Torphichen and Bathgate were, in that order, the largest providers.

As we will see in the following sections, from most parts of Scotland female migrants outnumbered the males: migration to Linlithgow from within the county fits the same pattern.

Women

Breaking down the female population of the parish by place of birth, the other parishes of West Lothian come second only to Linlithgow, ahead of any other Scottish county or the entirety of Ireland.

Of those incoming West Lothian women who worked, the highest proportion came to be servants: they were almost twice as likely to be a servant as a woman born in the parish. In all there were 91 so employed. The next largest group of women from the rest of the county were the 25 who worked in agriculture. Again, the proportion of incoming West Lothian women in this sector was more than twice as high as the proportion of local women. They had not all come to be labourers: three of them were farmers, while only one Linlithgow born woman so styled herself.

Between them, these two groups comprised the high majority of the incoming

West Lothian women workers. All other occupations combined only added up to 30, of which the largest groups were four dressmakers and four involved in retail. These last were all business women: a grocer, a small grocer, a spirit dealer and the town's bookseller and druggist. Not working, though they may have wished to be, were five paupers and two prisoners.

Men

Men from other parts of West Lothian made up just under 11% of the male workforce. The balance of the occupations they came to do was radically different from the work done by male natives to the town. Far and away the most common sector of work was agriculture with 85, or almost two in five of the group. This meant that a male West Lothian incomer was two and a half times more likely to work in agriculture than a male native. In fact a higher proportion of male West Lothian incomers worked in agriculture than men from any other area. As with the women, these men were not all agricultural labourers: seven of them were farmers. Male West Lothian incomers were also about 50% more likely than natives to be labourers or miners. We have seen that there was little history of mining within the parish, unlike other parts of the county, which may explain some of the difference in that sector.

West Lothian born incoming men were much less likely than the locals to be involved in the apprenticed trades of the town. While a respectable number were working as shoemakers, there were only two men involved in any of the related leather trades.[171]

The only other type of work in which West Lothian men were employed in disproportionately high numbers was construction, where twelve had found work. Of these men, seven were masons and an eighth worked for a mason. It was noted in the previous section that of all the building trades this was the one which had slipped most from the grip of Linlithgow born men.

Summary

It is no surprise that Linlithgow was a draw for men and women from the surrounding areas. The women came in large numbers to work as servants for the increasingly affluent tradesmen and professionals of the parish. They also played a large part in agriculture. They made a notable contribution to the upper

---

171   Nineteen, or 1 in 11 compared to 255 or 1 or 3 for Linlithgow born men.

reaches of society by providing seven business women: three farmers and four shop owners.

The apprenticeship system, so dominated by Linlithgow born men, may be one of the reasons why low numbers of men from other West Lothian parishes were to be found employed in the traditional trades. When men from the rest of the county did move into the parish it was generally to do manual work, often in the rural areas rather than the burgh. The chief exception was construction: in particular, these men made up a high percentage of the masons.

Place of Birth: Ireland

Incomers born in Ireland

	All	Aged 13+	Aged 0-12
Men	429	376	53
Women	284	227	57
Total	713	603	110

Though Irish migration to Scotland is most often associated with the west coast they also moved in substantial numbers to other parts of the country as work opportunities arose. The 1851 census tells us that 2,856 people of Irish birth were present in West Lothian. Of these, 713 were resident in Linlithgow Parish. Despite the greater distance they had had to travel, there were more people in the parish from Ireland than from any individual Scottish county other than West Lothian itself. The drivers behind Irish migration have already been outlined in Chapter 1. It should be remembered that the 1840s saw one of the greatest waves of migration as the island struggled through the great potato blight. The resultant famine was exacerbated by the protectionist Corn Laws which were repealed in 1846 allowing some relief to reach Ireland, though the famine continued until 1850. When the 1851 census was taken in Ireland it was found that the population was almost 20% lower than the 1841 total. In Linlithgow in 1851 we find 110 children who have been brought over from Ireland. The proportion of children to adults is much lower than for incomers from other parts of West Lothian or the neighbouring Scottish counties. This does not seem surprising and probably indicates that those who were willing to make the journey were more likely to be single or at least childless. Unlike incomers from West Lothian or the surrounding counties, the men outnumbered the women.

Studying the ages of the children born in Ireland gives us a point at which we know their parents were still living there. This suggests that migration of families to this area had fallen sharply in the last years of the 1840s:

Table 16. Children born in Ireland who were living in Linlithgow at the census date, by age

Child Age	Date of Birth	Number in Linlithgow
0	31/3/1850 - 30/3/1851	1
1	31/3/1849 – 30/3/1850	0
2	31/3/1848 – 30/3/1849	2
3	31/3/1847 – 30/3/1848	1
4	31/3/1846 – 30/3/1847	6
5	31/3/1845 – 30/3/1846	10
6	31/3/1844 – 30/3/1845	10
7	31/3/1843 – 30/3/1844	14
8	31/3/1842 – 30/3/1843	12
9	31/3/1841 – 30/3/1842	12
10	31/3/1840 – 30/3/1841	13
11	31/3/1839 – 30/3/1840	12
12	31/3/1838 – 30/3/1839	17

That said, this result may well be at odds with the date of arrival of those who had come without children (or whose children did not survive in 1851).

We have already noted that Irish born children were far less likely to attend school than either those born in Linlithgow or incomers from other parts of Scotland. Of the 51 boys aged between five and twelve only eight (15.7%) were recorded as scholars and of the 49 girls in the same age range only twelve were (24.5%). Roughly speaking, an Irish born boy was about one fifth as likely to be in school as one born in West Lothian while a girl was a third as likely. Predictably, the occupations they became involved in were generally those which were lower skilled and labour intensive.

Men

The dominant sector for Irish men was the railways. Of 270 men working on the railways, 206 of them were Irish. To put this in context, the second largest contingent on the railways was the sixteen from Inverness-shire followed by seven from Argyll – two other areas which were seeing large scale migration at this period. It is worth noting that this group was not simply made up of men who had been in the town since the construction of the railway ten years earlier: in the 1841 census Baillie found that the town population contained 76 Irish born labourers - a term which included all labouring work including railway work.

Irishmen were also found in substantial numbers working in the other occupations with a high manual component. A total of 84 worked in agriculture, or just over one in five of the Irishmen. Unlike men from Linlithgow, or the rest of West Lothian, none of them were farmers. Rather, they were exclusively labourers or farm servants. Sixteen Irishmen worked in mining or quarrying and fourteen were general labourers

The Irishmen had little involvement in the apprenticed trades. The only two notable areas where they managed to make an impact were as masons and, to a lesser extent, tailors. Thirteen were masons and one was a mason's labourer. This may have been a hangover from the period of railway construction. Three were tailors.

The calico printfield provided occupation for many of the young Irishmen in the town, perhaps a first occupation for the sons who had come over as children with their parents. In all there were thirteen of them working there and though two were aged 35 and 45 the rest were aged between ten and eighteen, with an average age of just over thirteen. The 45 year old, James McCulloch, was a calico printer and the only one of the thirteen to be in a skilled role.

The Irishmen had come to work: only one was unemployed (described as being of delicate health) and one was a pauper.

Against this picture of a large number of men who had made this journey willing to take on whatever manual work was available, we must remember that in 1851 no less a man than the Provost of Linlithgow, John Hardy, had been born in the Emerald Isle, even though his connection may have been slight.

Women

One of the most striking things about the Irishwomen is the numbers who were not employed. Given that many of them were married to men who were undertaking low paid work it would have seemed natural for a high proportion of them to be trying to bring in a second income. Of course it may be that many of them were trying but not succeeding. We know that at this time the number of those requiring poor relief in West Lothian remained stubbornly high compared to the rest of Scotland. We also know that the number of people recorded as paupers does not come close to matching the number of registered poor. It may be that a proportion of the Irishwomen without occupations were recipients (perhaps intermittently) of poor relief, though not actually recorded as paupers. In any event, we find that while 48% of Linlithgow born women are not employed and 51% of women incomers from other parts of West Lothian, the figure for Irish women is just over 52%. It may have been the case that while women from other places of origin generally worked if they had to, the Irishwomen generally worked if they could. Anti-Irish prejudice could have been a factor but the census data cannot throw any light on the subject.

Of those who did manage to find work the largest number, 32, were servants. Per head of the population, this is well below average for a group this size. An Irishwoman was less than half as likely to be working as a servant than an incoming woman from West Lothian or Stirlingshire.

The next largest contingent was the 22 who worked at the calico printfield. As with the Irishmen, these tended to be young: two thirds were under 20. Irishwomen were also over represented at the paper mill. Again, most of the nine were young with the majority being in their teens.

Not surprisingly, a number were to be found working in agriculture. Proportionately, an Irishwoman was more likely to be found working formally in agriculture than a woman from any other birthplace with the sole exception of West Lothian incomers. As with the men, they were all working in manual roles.

One area in which the Irishwomen were dominant was that of lodging house provision. Of the 26 in the town, fully half came from Ireland. In most cases their lodgers were also Irish, pointing to a strong community looking after its own.

The one other field in which Irishwomen were to be found in higher than average numbers was as dressmakers and seamstresses.

Summary

The Irish had come in large numbers to Linlithgow parish and turned their hands to whatever work was available. The railways provided work for by far the largest number of men. Others tended to work in the heavily manual areas. Irish women appear to have struggled to find work, though they dominated the lodging house sector and some were taken on as servants.

The Irish, probably more than any other group, struggled to break into the middle and upper reaches of society. However, they were willing to make a start by fitting into niches in the lower parts. Though the Irish were underrepresented in retail they were overrepresented amongst the hawkers and had the only two clothes brokers.

Given the links between poverty and crime, it is not surprising that half of the prisoners in the county jail were Irish. At the other end of the scale, it was noteworthy that an Irish-born provost was running the burgh.

Place of Birth: Midlothian

Incomers born in Midlothian

	All	Aged 13+	Aged 0-12
Men	195	151	46
Women	215	167	48
Total	410	328	94

We turn now to the neighbouring Scottish counties. Sizeable numbers of people had moved from Midlothian, Stirlingshire and Lanarkshire to Linlithgow parish. Of these Midlothian, with 410, was the place of birth of the largest contingent.

As with West Lothian incomers, though not to quite the same extent, the number of women exceeded the number of men.

Within Midlothian, Edinburgh was the single most common place of birth with 107 people, to which could be added people in a number of locations such as Leith, Stockbridge, Gorgie and Newhaven, which are now considered as part of the city. A substantial number had come from places which are part of the modern West Lothian, such as Kirknewton and West and Mid Calder.

Women

The proportion of women from Midlothian who were not employed is fractionally lower than for the Irishwomen. Similar though the percentages may be, the employment profile of the two groups is very different. In fact, in almost every area where Irishwomen were overrepresented, Midlothian women were underrepresented and vice versa. The differences start at the top of society where five Midlothian women were annuitants and thus had an independent income, a luxury not available to any Irishwoman. Four were teachers, more than all other places of birth put together. One was an independent business woman - a spirit dealer and publican.

Midlothian women were amongst the most likely to be working as servants. A total of 42, or one in four, Midlothian women were in service, against one in five across all places of birth. Only seven Midlothian women were formally employed in agriculture, a below average proportion. No Midlothian women worked at the calico printfield (though there were two tambourers) and only one at the paper mill.

The one sector of employment in which the Midlothian women and the Irishwomen found themselves working in similar numbers was the making of clothes. Midlothian was the place of birth of six dressmakers and two seamstresses. A milliner and a straw bonnet maker also hailed from Midlothian.

Men

Midlothian men were employed across a broad range of areas. Their employment profile is not dissimilar to West Lothian incomers, which is not surprising given that many came from communities that are now within the area administered by the present-day West Lothian Council.

The largest group was the 45, only one of whom came from Edinburgh, who worked in agriculture. This meant that a Midlothian man was proportionally more likely than anyone other than a West Lothian incomer to work in this sector. Six of the 45 were farmers.

The next largest group were fifteen shoemakers followed by thirteen labourers – both numbers are similar to those for West Lothian incomers.

Midlothian provided nine woodworkers, the biggest contingent outside

Linlithgow itself. Most were joiners or carpenters but one was Charles Douglas, the town's only cabinet maker.

As noted in the section on paper manufacture, the town had imported half (four of the eight) of its skilled paper makers from Midlothian. Amongst the minor occupations, two other areas where Midlothian had provided notable proportions of people were gardening (five of the parish's eighteen) and rope making (three of the five).

One area where Midlothian men are conspicuous by their absence is construction with only three representatives.

At the upper reaches of society, Midlothian was the birth place of William Sheils, Rector of the Grammar School, and John Baillie, Minister of the Free Church of Scotland.

Summary

For men in particular, the employment pattern of Midlothian born people had much in common with that of people born in the other parishes of West Lothian. They were strongly represented in agriculture, both as farm labourers and as farmers. They had not made inroads into the apprenticed professions, though they were as well represented as any incomers in shoemaking. Like the women, Midlothian men were well represented in the professions, especially education. Midlothian women appear to have been relatively affluent. They were underrepresented in the less desirable work areas, such as agriculture, and textile and paper manufacture, and overrepresented in more desirable ones such as service and dress and hat making.

Place of Birth: Stirlingshire

Incomers born in Stirlingshire

	All	Aged 13+	Aged 0-12
Men	118	83	35
Women	198	163	35
Total	316	246	70

The eastern parts of Stirlingshire are closer to Linlithgow than the southern parts of West Lothian. Also, Linlithgow had good transport links to Stirlingshire with the town lying on the road from Stirling to Edinburgh. It is therefore not surprising that a substantial number of people born in Stirlingshire were living in Linlithgow in 1851. We find that women have come in particularly large numbers, outnumbering the men by almost two to one.

Many people had come from the closest parishes. Neighbouring Muiravonside was the birthplace of 94 people. Moving westward, Polmont accounted for 29 people and Falkirk for 60. Between them these three made up 58% of the Stirlingshire total.

Women

The percentage of Stirlingshire women in employment was almost identical to those from Midlothian. Beyond that, there were similarities in the pattern of their employment to that of women from both Midlothian and the other parishes of West Lothian. Like them, Stirlingshire provided disproportionately high numbers of servants: 47 were employed in this way. Unlike Midlothian, an above average number of Stirlingshire women worked in agriculture. This was largely thanks to Muiravonside – birthplace of seven of the nine.

There are no other notable clusters of employment in the Stirlingshire women. What we see instead is a series of small numbers – one to four – spread across most sectors. Of these, the largest group is four shopkeepers.

Men

Like the women, Stirlingshire men were also well spread across the range of occupations. There were some notable features worth exploring. Stirlingshire men, and in particular those from Muiravonside, played an important role in agriculture. Over a quarter of incoming men from that county worked in this sector, rising to over a third of those from Muiravonside.[172] More significantly, eight Stirlingshire born people were farmers, of whom five came from Muiravonside. This meant that, aside from those born within Linlithgow parish itself, a farm was more likely to be in the hands of someone from Stirlingshire than anywhere else.

---

172   23 and 11 respectively.

Muiravonside men were also at the heart of two other areas in which we find disproportionately high numbers from Stirlingshire: fleshing and general labouring. Of the eleven fleshers in the town five came from Muiravonside. Indeed, Stirlingshire people made a notable contribution to trade in general. As well as the fleshers and the four women shopkeepers the county provided a grocer, a grain dealer and a corn merchant/grocer. Turning to general labouring, seven Stirlingshire men earned their living this way – a proportionately higher number than any of the major areas other than Midlothian.

Summary

Incomers from Stirlingshire could be found in a wide range of employment, broadly similar to incomers from Midlothian. Women who worked were likely to be servants and were also present in above average numbers in agriculture (a contrast with Midlothian). The men also had a high involvement in agriculture. Seven men and one woman gave their occupation as farmers. The people of Muiravonside were particularly active in the Linlithgow agricultural community. Looking more widely, there were Muiravonside born farmers in a number of the other West Lothian parishes including Bathgate, Bo'ness, Torphichen and Whitburn.

Muiravonside provided half the town's fleshers. As with farming Muiravonside fleshers can be found in a number of other West Lothian parishes suggesting that this was a trade with a strong tradition in that parish. As well as fleshing, Stirlingshire men and women were involved in above average numbers in the town's retail activities.

Place of Birth: Lanarkshire

Incomers born in Lanarkshire

	All	Aged 13+	Aged 0-12
Men	70	52	18
Women	96	63	33
Total	166	115	51

As table 18 shows, Lanarkshire was the last Scottish county to provide over 100 people to Linlithgow parish. In the same way that the figures for Midlothian were dominated by people from Edinburgh, so those from Lanarkshire are dominated by Glasgow, and the neighbouring areas that we now think of as being part of the city. In total, 86 people in Linlithgow parish had been born in Glasgow itself. The north of Lanarkshire had undergone an economic transformation in the second quarter of the nineteenth century with mining and heavy industry causing towns such as Airdrie to mushroom in size. Even as they sucked in large numbers of people, some were leaving. Some of the data shows a lack of knowledge on the part of the Linlithgow Census Enumerators of a relatively nearby area: there are people shown as having been born in the parishes of Monkland, New Monkland, Old Monkland and Airdrie. In fact, these places were all part of two parishes: New Monkland, which contained Airdrie, and Old Monkland, which contained Coatbridge. Collecting the related entries together, we find 33 people from this area. A further thirteen had come from Shotts. As usual with the neighbouring counties, the number of women who had moved to Linlithgow was markedly higher than the number of men.

Women

Fifteen Lanarkshire women were employed as servants. Proportionally this put them below the other neighbouring counties but above the average for all areas. The area of employment in which Lanarkshire women stand out as being highly represented is calico printing. Nine Lanarkshire 'women' (four of them were under twelve) worked at the printfield. Proportionally, a Lanarkshire woman was far more likely to work there than a woman from any other area. Indeed there were as many Lanarkshire women working at the printfield as there were in total from Stirlingshire, Midlothian and the other West Lothian parishes.

At the other end of the social scale, three of the parish's eight female house proprietors came from Lanarkshire.

No Lanarkshire women worked in agriculture or in retail related activities. The former is not unsurprising given that many of them had urban origins.

Men

As with the women, a Lanarkshire man was proportionally more likely than a man from any other area to work in textiles. Though the total number (six) was not in itself extraordinary what is distinctive is that no other area of employment had more Lanarkshire men in it. In every other neighbouring county the largest number of incomers had found employment in agriculture. Lanarkshire had a tradition of weaving beginning well before the establishment of New Lanark. Lanarkshire men, like the women, tended not to come from rural areas and only five men were working in the agricultural sector. Under shoemaking we noted the rise of large scale production in the Bridgeton area of Glasgow. This may be the reason for the presence of six Lanarkshire shoemakers in Linlithgow, four of whom had come from the city.

No other area of employment attracted substantial numbers of Lanarkshire men: the remainder were well spread across the range of sectors.

Summary

Incomers from Lanarkshire came in higher proportions to the town rather than the rural parts of the parish. The men were only involved in agriculture in small numbers and the women not at all. Both sexes were disproportionately involved in calico printing. For men, calico printing and shoemaking were the major employers. For women being a servant was the most common employment, as it was for all the major providers of population. However, Lanarkshire woman were employed as servants in a lower proportion than those from any of the other neighbouring areas.

Place of Birth: The Highlands and Islands

Professor T. C. Smout wrote that 'The Highland clearances reached a peak in the 1840s and first part of the 1850s, especially in the aftermath of the great potato blight of 1846, which saw upwards of 100,000 people in the north-west destitute and dependent on the charity of relief funds to keep them from starvation.'[173]

This serves as a useful reminder that it was not only the Irish that suffered from the potato blight and shows that 1851 fell within a key period in the story of the depopulation of the Highlands and Islands.

In the census we find 83 people within the parish of Linlithgow who had been born in, Argyll, Inverness-shire, Ross & Cromarty, Sutherland and Caithness.[174]

---

173   *Smout, ACOTSP, p62*
174   *There were no incomers born in Orkney or Shetland.   Inverness-shire and Ross & Cromarty included Skye and the Western Isles.*

Incomers born in the Highlands and Islands

	All	Aged 13+	Aged 0-12
Men	53	52	1
Women	30	26	4
Total	83	78	5

In many respects the group from the Highlands & Islands (henceforth the Highlands, or Highlanders) most resembles the Irish. Only 15% of the Irish population of Linlithgow parish were children in contrast with incomers from West Lothian, Midlothian, Stirlingshire and Lanarkshire where the figure ranged from 20-30%. The figure for the Highlands was even lower at 6%. Amongst the adults, men outnumbered women by two to one.

With only five children it is difficult to draw firm conclusions, but it is worth noting that the youngest is five years old. As with the Irish, this would suggest a fall off in migration to the area after 1846. Interestingly, and in contrast to the Irish, all Highland children were recorded as scholars.

Men

Highland men typically found employment in the heavy manual occupations. A total of 28 of the men were railway labourers, a further four were general labourers while three were quarrymen and one was a brewer's labourer. Only two worked in agriculture and they were both shepherds.

Almost all the rest were employed across a number of traditional trades: three shoe makers, two curriers, two masons, two joiners, a carpenter and a gardener. The remaining men were the missionary, Adam Gordon, a fourteen year old 'man' who was still at school and a visiting railway labourer from the Island of Eigg.

Women

We have seen that Irish women seem to have struggled to find employment. This appears to have been even more the case for Highland women. Despite having husbands who generally had low paid employment and being relatively unencumbered with children, fourteen (54 %) of Highland women have no occupation recorded against them on top of which two (8%) were paupers. Of the ten who were working, eight were servants (including a housekeeper and a cook), one was an agricultural labourer and one was a lodging house keeper. This last was Elizabeth Donaly, 33, from Thurso who lived at 51 High Street with her one year old son and three lodgers (the McGrivie family from Ireland).

Summary

Railway labouring was the major employment for men from the Highlands while a number of men worked in other labouring jobs. However, for their number, Highland men were relatively well represented in the traditional trades.

Highland women were less likely even than Irish women to be in employment. Almost all who were in work were servants.

Place of Birth: Other Scottish Counties

Incomers born in other Scottish Counties (not neighbouring, not Highlands & Islands)

	All	Aged 13+	Aged 0-12
Men	180	136	44
Women	218	169	49
Total	398	305	93

Though there are variations on a county by county basis the other Scottish counties (i.e., those which are neither neighbouring to West Lothian nor in the Highlands and Islands) are considered together as a group for two reasons. Firstly, the numbers from individual counties are generally so small that they make it difficult to reach clear conclusions. Secondly, in looking at their data in aggregate, it is clear that the employment pattern for people from these counties is somewhat different from any of the other groups. By pulling the data together we get a group of people (henceforth 'Other Scots') slightly smaller than the number which had come from Midlothian.

In some ways the data is similar to that of Linlithgow's neighbouring counties: women slightly outnumber men and about a quarter of the population are children. It is when the employment data is broken down that differences start to appear.

Women

The first major difference between the data for the neighbouring counties and the Other Scots is that a remarkable number did not work, nearly 60%. Six of them appear to have had independent income, a higher number per head of population than any group other than the English (due largely to one family - for details see below) and more than twice the average for all women in Linlithgow. They were also more likely than average to be involved in retail and three of them ran their own businesses.

As usual, amongst those who worked the largest group (35) were servants. Proportionally this is almost exactly average for all women living in Linlithgow. There were no other large concentrations and it is most revealing to look at the employment areas in which they are underrepresented. Going back to Table 6 we see that the top five employment areas for women in the parish were as servants, in agriculture, calico printing, dressmaking and tambouring. We have already covered the first of these. In agriculture they barely feature (four). Only five worked at the calico print field, less than half the female average, there was one dressmaker (from East Lothian) and no tambourers.

Men

The male data confirm the pattern suggested in the women's data that many of those who had come from the non-neighbouring, non-Highland counties belonged to the more prosperous sections of society. The number who were railway labourers was low (five) and not a single one was a general labourer. Only twelve of the men were working in agriculture, less than half the average for this size of population.

Turning again to Table 6, the above covers three of the top five male spheres of employment, the other two being shoemaking and calico printing. Taking the second of these first there were only two men who worked at the printfield. Shoemaking, the most skilled of the five occupations, was in fact the largest single employer of Other Scots men with thirteen, while a further six were employed in the related leather trades. Looking at the other apprenticed trades, Other Scots men were overrepresented amongst the masons, wood workers and paper makers.

The most disproportionately large contributions made by Other Scots men were to the professional occupations. In particular five of the town's ministers and four of the teachers came from the other counties.

Summary

The employment profile suggests that people from the non-neighbouring, non-Highland counties who had moved to Linlithgow were, on average, more affluent than other Scottish groups. In particular they were far less likely to be employed in manual or low skilled occupations. Women, if they worked at all, were most likely to be servants. The men dominated the town's pulpits and classrooms. They were found in most of the traditional skilled professions in proportions that were only exceeded by Linlithgow born men.

Place of Birth: England

Incomers born in England

	All	Aged 13+	Aged 0-12
Men	29	24	5
Women	38	33	5
Total	67	57	10

On the night of the 1851 census Linlithgow contained 67 people born in England. This was similar to the number of residents who had been born in the county of Fife or the parish of Abercorn. Unfortunately, in most cases the county of birth was not recorded but in any case it is clear that a move to Linlithgow is not something that would have been undertaken lightly given the distance travelled and, presumably in most cases at least, the degree of separation this would imply from family and friends.

The English brought with them a relatively small number of English born children. An examination of their occupations sheds some light on this. Once again we see that the women outnumber the men.

Women

Of the 33 adult English women, 24 can be excluded from the ranks of those who worked. Fifteen have no occupation recorded, two were annuitants, three were visitors, one was a prisoner and three were gentlewomen. This last group were Elizabeth Lake (58), Isabella Lake (31) and a second Elizabeth Lake (30), all resident at the Star & Garter. One may guess that Elizabeth the elder was the mother or aunt of the two younger Lakes. Janet Bell (annuitant, 36) lived with her English sister-in-law, Mary McKenzie Stein (of whom more in a moment). The other annuitant, 85 year old Elizabeth Miller, lived with her brother-in-law, James Melville, a tax collector born in Canada.

Of the nine who worked, six could be described as servants (a slightly below average figure even if all six are accepted within the category), but the profile of the group is very different from the norm. Though one fifteen year old was a house servant, two were housekeepers and three were governesses. This last group are difficult to categorise. They comprised the aforementioned Mary McKenzie Stein and two more of her sisters-in-law, Anne and Marion Stein. A governess would normally be expected to be a live-in servant, as we find with the only two other governesses in the West Lothian census for the year. The Stein governesses lived at 40 High Street, where Mary was head of the household even though the residents included her mother and artist father. Though Mary gave her occupation as a governess in 1851, a year later in Slater we see her listed as one of the individual educators under 'Academies and Schools'. Perhaps having come north to look after her parents, hoping to find work as a governess, she had decided to set up in business with two of her sisters-in-law, offering private tuition.

While we are considering servants it seems appropriate to mention the one Englishman in that category. As with the women, he was a servant of a superior type – he was the butler at Binny House.

Men

Alone of all the geographical groups we have considered, Englishmen were most likely to work as what one might loosely term civil servants in that their pay would come from the state. Four were tax collectors, two worked at the prison and one was a letter carrier. We have already noted that the English dominated tax collecting within not just the town but the county. The prison was run by an English couple and an English warder.

The other men were scattered across a variety of occupations. Though there was one railway labourer, one calico printer's tearer and one prisoner, the rest were in higher skilled professions. Mention should be made off John Kirsopp who had established himself in the town not just as a draper but also as a magistrate. The dates of birth of his seven children indicate that he had been in Linlithgow for at least sixteen years.

Summary

Many of the English people in Linlithgow had come to fulfil specialised or higher status roles. The tax collectors and prison staff may have worked as part of national organisations, which resulted in them moving around the country as part of their careers.

Employment By Birth Place – Conclusions

Just over half of the population of the Linlithgow parish, and 43% of the adult population, were born within the parish. In the period from 1841 to 1851 the population of the burgh had increased by 199 while that of the rest of the parish had gone down by 34. From this it might have been expected that the main flow of migrants was into the town. However, we know that across the parish agriculture was the biggest single employer and that two thirds of those who worked in agriculture were incomers. Mining and quarrying employed 62 men, a not insubstantial number, of whom two thirds (again) were incomers. Like agriculture, this was an occupation which took place outside the boundaries of the burgh, although some of the practitioners could, and did, live within it. Set against a situation where the rural population had suffered a slight decline, these figures suggest that, while there had been considerable migration into the countryside, this had been more than offset by locals moving on, either into the town or further afield out of the parish. A substantial majority of this migration into the rural parts of the parish came from other West Lothian parishes and the surrounding counties of Midlothian, Stirlingshire and Lanarkshire. This was not just a movement of the labouring classes: many local farms had changed hands and were owned by men (and women) from the same locations.

The Irish also provided a substantial number of agricultural labourers and not a few miners and quarrymen. However, their main role in the economy was keeping the railways running. In this task they were joined in smaller numbers by men from the Highlands and Islands.

Not all labouring skills lay outside the town. There were general labourers as well and a mix of low and high skilled jobs in calico printing and at the paper mill. The birthplace pattern for general labourers was similar to that for agriculture. At the printfield and the paper mill the low skilled jobs tended to go to young locals (usually under 20) or to Irish migrants.

The economy of the town was built around the traditional trades, especially shoemaking. In the main, these had stayed in local hands, though domination of the masons had been well and truly lost and the tailors were evenly divided between locals and incomers. While small numbers of skilled incomers were able to find work in the trades, the masters were generally locals and so were the apprentices, ensuring continued control.

If the apprenticeship system was in effect a barrier to entry, there were some areas of the urban economy, such as trade, retail and dressmaking, where the locals were not able to exert the same control. In particular, traders from nearby areas seem to have found it relatively easy to set up within the town since the passing of the Burgh Trading Act in 1846.

Incomers from the other Scottish counties (non-neighbouring, non-Highlands and Islands) tended to be more affluent, to have come for a specific opportunity. Linlithgow at this time seems to have been unable to produce its own teachers and ministers, although they dominated the legal profession. The other Scottish counties filled the gap.

To sum up, migrants undertaking largely manual work tended to come a short distance: from the rest of West Lothian and the neighbouring counties. In general, where people had travelled greater distances they tend to be found in higher skilled or status jobs. The exceptions to this pattern were the Irish and the Highlanders. Fleeing great hardship rather than seeking out greater opportunities, they tended to fill the gaps at the bottom of the labour market that the Scots were not inclined to undertake. Gaps at the top of society were generally filled by skilled men from other parts of Scotland.

For all the geographical groupings considered, it is only from Ireland and the Highlands that the number of male incomers exceeded the number of women. Many of the women were not employed in 1851. In the case of the Irish and Highland women the suspicion, based on the occupations of the men, is that they were unable to find work whereas this seems less likely for the wives of more affluent incomers. The great attraction for women was the opportunity to go into service: roughly 40% of all the working women in the parish were servants. The areas which supplied these in the highest proportions were, again, other

West Lothian parishes and the neighbouring counties. Female servants, however, could be found from all round Scotland, as well as Ireland and even a few from England.

Overall, the degree of population movement at this time is striking. The reality is far from the picture of a population living and dying in the same place their parents and grandparents had lived before them. The alternative picture of the poor country boy heading off to the town to find a new life holds some truth, but only for those areas of the country which had suffered the greatest deprivation in the preceding years.[175] In fact, the evidence tells us that an independent young Scots woman was more likely than her male counterpart to have found herself a job (though admittedly from a more limited range) and moved away from home to Linlithgow.

The defining features of the labour force of Linlithgow parish in 1851 were flexibility and pluralism. It is clear many business and trades people diversified into multiple areas, sometimes creating unlikely combinations of interests. There was also an important informal and seasonal sector which saw men women and children respond to the changing needs of the economy. That said, in many ways the labour market appears to have been sophisticated and relocation was routine: more akin to today's world than might have been expected. This was an age where teachers, ministers and civil servants found their way to Linlithgow from all parts of Scotland and England. This was an age where the Star & Garter would be advertised in the Glasgow Herald and taken over by a man from Dunbar in a matter of weeks.

---

175   *And in Linlithgow parish he is as likely to have moved into the countryside as the town.*

CHAPTER FIVE
AFTERWARDS

The coming of the railways provided great threats and opportunities for the manufacturers of Linlithgow. We have seen that, first the canal and then the railways made the extraction and export of raw materials increasingly economically viable. Nearby, Falkirk was transformed by the railway: between 1842 and 1875, five new iron foundries were established,[176] resulting in the rapid growth of the town and a shift in economic power in the locality.

A new energy source was about to have a big impact on the town. In Slater we find Robert Carlow, a blacksmith in the 1851 census, had, by 1852, become manager of the Gas Light Company on Vennel Green. This was a new technology and it took a number of years to be adopted, but in 1860 Linlithgow was to become one of the first towns in Scotland to be lit by gas.[177] The next great leap, to electricity, was a source of debate in the town in 1901.[178]

We know from the first and second Statistical Accounts that the care of the needy in society had been a difficult issue for many years. This had been exacerbated by the split in the Church of Scotland. The Scottish Poor Law Act of 1845 gave parishes the option of combining together to operate a single poorhouse, often called a Combination Poorhouse. In 1854, after several years of discussion, the Linlithgow poorhouse was built. Described as 'a notable Scottish Baronial building',[179] it cost £9000. With accommodation for up to 230 people, it catered for the poor of Abercorn, Bathgate, Bo'ness, Carriden, Kirkliston, Linlithgow, Muiravonside and Whitburn.[180]

The Ordnance Gazetteer of Scotland (published in 1884) gives us a snapshot of the town 33 years after our period. Describing the industries of the town it says:

> 'In the end of the last century the staple industries were wool-combing, tanning and shoemaking.' Then 'Tanning, currying and shoemaking may still be looked on as the staple industries, and in or near the town are two paper - mills, two distilleries, a soap work, and sawmills, while extensive shale works have been established in the district.'[181]

The shale works had dramatically shifted the economic centre of gravity away

---

176   Thomas, p67
177   Jamieson, p3
178   Linlithgowshire Gazette, 3rd May 1901, p6
179   Groome, p520
180   Groome, p520
181   Groome, p520

from Linlithgow to the south of the county.

The Ordnance Gazetteer also gives us a window into social life in the town in 1884, noting a bowling club, a bicycle club, a curling club, a company of volunteers (riflemen), a horticultural society, a mechanics' institute, a workingmen's club and a workingmen's hall.[182]

The Calico Print Works had already come to grief before the writing of the Ordnance Gazetteer. In the late 1850s Britain suffered from the 'Cotton Famine'. The death knell for the industry in the town was the opening of hostilities in the American Civil War in 1860. That year the print works was converted to paper making.

Though not mentioned in the Ordnance Gazetteer, 1884 was also to see the revival of an old industry in a new form. The first Statistical Account had reported fishing as a significant element with the town's economy. Nearly a century later, Mr Anderson, an Edinburgh fishmonger, set up a salmon hatchery on the loch.[183]

Avon Mills, J Lovell & Sons, Paper makers 1870-1971. Copyright Sandy Thomson

---

182   Groome, p520
183   Glasgow Herald, 21st March 1884

By 1901 many of the smaller trades had ceased to be practised in the town. The author of the series of articles in the Gazette on Linlithgow in 1851 singled out shoemaking as a continuing success:

> 'The leather industry, so prominent fifty years ago, is still to-day in most capable and energetic hands, and bids fair to flourish more prosperously yet in the years to come.'[184]

In fact shoemaking's ascendancy was to last only another two decades. W L Morrison Shoe Company was the last local business with a connection to the cordiners of the Victorian period. Morrison ceased shoe production in the 1950s[185] and ceased trading as a shoe shop during the writing of this book. Of the industries and trades prominent in 1851, paper making was to prove the longest lasting: it was to remain a major employer up until the early 1970s.

---

184   *Linlithgowshire Gazette, 3rd May 1901, p6.*
185   *Linlithgow Old and New, p75*

BIBLIOGRAPHY

The principal source for this work was the 1851 Census. I am grateful to the West Lothian Family History Society for their transcription some years ago of the records onto CD which greatly speeded up the data processing.

Principle Sources

Andrina Baillie, 'Linlithgow in Early Victorian Times', West Lothian Council Local History Library, 2006

The Linlithgowshire Gazette, 'Linlithgow in 1851', a series of four articles printed from 12/04/1901 to 3/05/1901

'The New Statistical Account, Volume 2', Edinburgh, 1834-45

Pigot & Co. Trade Directory, 1837

Sir John Sinclair (editor), 'The Statistical Account of Scotland, Volume 14', Edinburgh, 1791-99

Slater's Commercial Trade Directory for Scotland, 1852

Additional Sources

George F. Black, 'The Surnames of Scotland', Birlinn Limited, 1993 (original publication by the New your Public Library, 1946)

David Bremner, 'The Industries of Scotland', Adam and Charles Black, 1869, reprinted 1969

G. I. Brown, 'The Guinness History of Inventions', Guinness Publishing, 1996

John Butt, 'The Industrial Archaeology of Scotland', 1967

G. D. H. Cole, 'A Short History of the British Working-Class Movement 1789-1947 ' George Allen & Unwin, 1948

B. Collins, 'The Irish in Britain 1780-1921', in B. Graham & G. Proudfoot (editors) "An Historical Geography of Ireland" London, 1993

A Dawson, 'Rambling Recollections of Past Times', Falkirk, 1868

E Patricia Dennison & Russel Coleman, 'Historic Linlithgow', Historic Scotland, 2000

Michael Flinn (editor), 'Scottish Population History from the Seventeenth Century to the 1930s', Cambridge University Press, 1977

Gardiner & Wenborn (editors), 'The History Today Companion to British History', Collins & Brown, 1995

Francis H. Groome (editor), 'Ordnance Gazetteer of Scotland Volume V', Grange Publishing Works, Edinburgh 1884

James Handley, 'The Irish in Modern Scotland' 1947

Bruce Jamieson, 'Old Linlithgow', Stenlake Publishing, 1998

James Lothian, 'History of John Wright the Joiner', Northern Warder Office, Dundee, 1855

John & Julia Keay (editors), 'Collins Encyclopaedia of Scotland', Harper Collins, 1994

Angus & Alison Mitchell, 'West Lothian Monumental Inscriptions (Pre 1855), Volume 2', The Scottish Genealogy Society, 2006

Philip's World History Encyclopedia, George Philip's Limited, 2000

George Bartlett Prescott, 'History, Theory, and Practice of the Electric Telegraph' Ticknor and Fields, 1860

John Shaw, 'Water Power in Scotland 1550-1870', John Donald, 1984

Ron Smith (editor), 'Linlithgow Old and New', Linlithgow Civic Trust, 2002

T. C. Smout, 'A Century of the Scottish People 1830-1950', Fontana Press, 1986

T. C. Smout, 'A History of the Scottish People 1560-1830', Fontana Press, 1969

John Thomas, 'A Regional History of the Railways Volume VI', 1971

A. J. Younger, 'The Making of Classical Edinburgh', Edinburgh University Press, 1966

APPENDIX

Statistical findings

Table 17. Residents of Linlithgow in 1851 born in West Lothian - by parish

Linlithgow	3211
Bo'ness	121
Kirkliston	83
Torphichen	80
Bathgate	75
Abercorn	62
Uphall	52
Carriden	50
Ecclesmachan	30
Livingston	25
Dalmeny	24
Whitburn	18
Queensferry	7
Unknown	18

Table 18. Residents of Linlithgow in 1851 - by county place of birth

West Lothian	3856
Midlothian	410
Stirling	316
Lanark	166
Perth	75
Fife	70
East Lothian	41
Renfrew	40
Berwick	34
Argyll	31
Ayr	30

Dunbarton	30
Inverness	29
Roxburgh	26
Dumfries	21
Kinross	19
Aberdeen	14
Forfar	14
Peebles	12
Ross & Cromarty	12
Clackmannan	11
Moray	10
Wigtown	9
Sutherland	6
Scotland	5
Selkirk	5
Kirkcudbright	4
Kincardine	3
Banff	2
Caithness	2
Nairn	2
Bute	1
Orkney	0
Shetland	0

Table 19. Residents of Linlithgow in 1851 born outwith Scotland

Ireland	713
England	67
Wales	0
Canada	2
United States	2
East Indies	1

France	1
Italy	1
Illegible	3
Unknown	16

Table 20. Boys and Girls at School and Work in Linlithgow, 1851 with 'core' school years highlighted

Age	% Boys Scholars	% Boys Working	% Girls Scholars	% Girls Working
1	0	0	0	0
2	3	0	0	0
3	6	0	4	0
4	13	0	21	0
5	46	0	29	0
6	82	0	70	0
7	80	0	75	5
8	83	0	77	0
9	79	3	83	3
10	71	15	77	6
11	65	19	70	8
12	64	21	45	20
13	31	62	33	43
14	26	61	28	44
15	11	81	16	59
16	7	85	8	63
17	2	98	0	80
18	3	93	1	71

Fig 5. Percentage of boys at school and in work by age

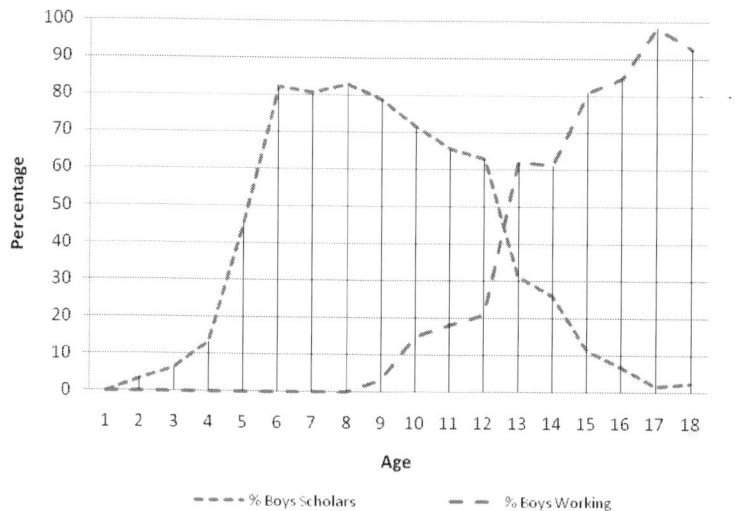

Fig 6. Percentage of girls at school and in work by age

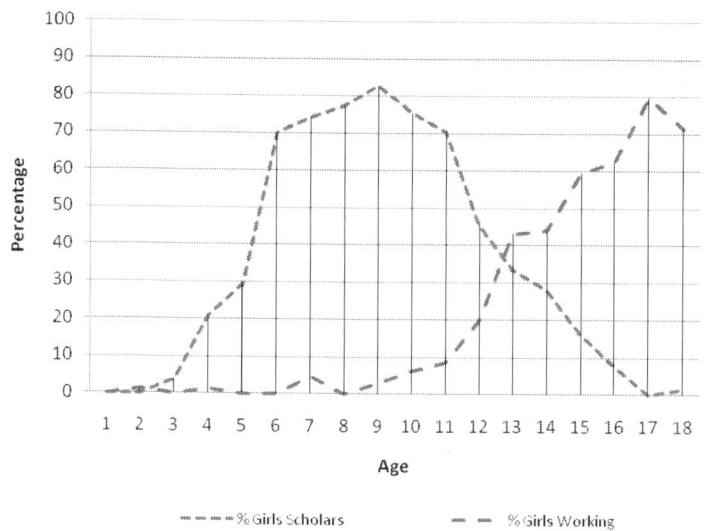

INDEX

Printed in Great Britain
by Amazon